Seeing Through
The 12 Biggest Obstacles To
Enlightenment

David A. Bhodan

<u>Right Now</u>
Publishing

Right Now Publishing

ISBN-13: 978-1505999068
ISBN-10: 1505999065

Copyright © 2014 by David A. Bhodan

All Rights Reserved. No part of this publication may be reproduced in any form or by any means, including scanning, photocopying, recording, taping, or by an information storage retrieval system (or otherwise) without prior written permission of the copyright holder.

First Printing, 2015

Printed in the United States of America

Table of Contents

Preface	i
Curiosity Didn't Kill This Cat	iii
Chapter 1 — Lighten Up, Francis	1
Chapter 2 — The Devil You Know	14
Chapter 3 — Dancing With The Dead	22
Chapter 4 — Seek And Don't Find	31
Chapter 5 — No Path To Now	37
Chapter 6 — Ignoring Direct Experience	43
Chapter 7 — It Can't Be *That* Simple!	52
Chapter 8 — Even More Than Fear	58
Chapter 9 — Caught In Dualism	67
Chapter 10 — Hey, Where Did I Go?	77
Chapter 11 — Guru Speak And Jive Talk	82
Chapter 12 — A Sense Of A Separate Self	95
In A Nutshell	104

Dedication

This book is dedicated to my teachers, Adyashanti and Prajna Ginty. You held up a lantern, pointed me towards liberation until it was seen. Doubt, being the last thing to go, was forever removed.

It is nothing I ever imagined; little did I know that This is nothing I *could* imagine. The chains have been long gone. You have my eternal gratitude.

This is a book about Seeing Who You Really Are.
Most aren't ready for this message.

Are You?

Ponder This

If the cause of all your problems is completely removed from your experience, what must happen to the effects?

If the cause of all your problems is your belief in the "I" thought, then what must happen to the effects that this imagined "I" thought creates when it's seen through?

All your struggles, insecurities, and psychological and emotional suffering dissolve in the Formless Light of Consciousness YOU ARE.

This is True Freedom.

This is What You Are.

Preface

After publishing, *"The Lazy Man's Way To Enlightenment: What You're Looking For Is What Is Looking"*, it occurred to me that most will still need to do more investigation into the discovery of Who They Really Are. And in that investigation, the mind will undoubtedly begin to throw up roadblock after roadblock. Why does it do this? Put simply, the mind doesn't want You to remember Who You Really Are. In fact, it fears this immensely, because if You do, no longer would it be the Master. Being all about survival and control, no longer would it be running the show. And this notion is downright scary to the mind.

Still believing you are the mind, you'll think these roadblocks are real – and you'll see things that are not there. Identified with the mind as who you are, it is only natural to believe that these obstructions must be 'overcome' if awakening is to happen. Identified with the mind and body as who you are, it makes perfect sense that you'll believe these mind-created obstacles are in need of overcoming. But they aren't. In reality, there isn't anything in the way of Seeing Who You Really Are, at least not anything real. Some of these seeming obstacles (or all of them) will have you feeling stuck and confused.

And so, while there isn't anything to overcome in order to recognize what you've always been, there are definitely some things to see through – not by the mind, but by YOU. *"Seeing Through The 12 Biggest Obstacles To Enlightenment"* contains 12 of the most common obstacles that postpone the realization of your True Identity. The truth is, the real YOU is already seeing through the 12 obstacles presented in this book (they aren't even present), but if you haven't yet seen through the illusion of the separate self, you'll identify with these obstacles. But before you read this book, it is worth reiterating: there aren't any actual obstacles in the way of realizing who you really are.

The last thing I want to do here is set it up in the mind that real obstacles exist. They do not. However, the mind is very astute in the art of delay tactics and postponement strategies, so that you don't see who you really are. Creating seeming obstacles that aren't real is one of the many tactics it uses. And so, if you want to enjoy a beautiful sunset, you must face (and look) in the direction of West. However, if you're facing and looking East, you miss out on the beauty and majesty that the sunset offers. This book is about noticing *when you*'re facing East, in order to reorient yourself in the direction of West, so you can LOOK West, where your freedom lies.

David A. Bhodan
November - 2014

Curiosity Didn't Kill This Cat

When you're driving down the road and you see the flashing lights of police cars and ambulances stopped on the side of the road, don't you slow down and look to see how serious the accident was?

Or perhaps who was in the accident?

You may almost hit the car in front of you, or the car coming at you from the opposite direction, but out of intense curiosity, you're compelled to look.

When you hear a loud noise, don't you generally turn in the direction of where you think it came from in the hope of identifying the source of that noise? It could be during the night while you're sleeping, while you're walking down the street in the middle of the day, or even now, while reading this paragraph.

The point is you just have to know *what* is making that sound, don't you?

How about when you hear a beautiful piece of music on the radio, don't you generally want to know who the composer/singer/musician is? I know I do.

If you're like most people, you possess a natural tendency to be curious about a lot of things. It's just the way you're wired. And if you look, you'll notice that you don't consciously decide to *be* curious.

Curiosity just arises, naturally and spontaneously.

It is much like thinking. If you look and see, you'll also notice that you don't decide to think, but that thinking happens all by itself. This recognition alone, seen clearly, can dramatically alter your entire perception of reality to the point where it is no longer 'your' perception.

And so, there is the kind of curiosity that arises spontaneously, and then there is the kind of curiosity that stems from a conscious intention to place your focus on something you want to know more about, because if you remain in the status quo, not much will change.

When we give ourselves permission to ask questions and relax into the unknown, we sometimes become aware of things we weren't aware of before – and it's what we presently aren't aware of that keeps us stuck in the familiar.

Asking ourselves, "Is it true?" is one of the most powerful questions we can ask. It is the one question that reveals things to you that you never thought possible.

The desire to find out what you really are comes from a deep integrity that won't settle for anything less than truth.

You can't manufacture this desire.

And it is this integrity that cuts through our illusions that keep us on the wheel of suffering.

Those who keep their illusions can do so and remain frozen in place. Those who fear them will fall into safer illusions. Those who see through them will let wisdom bloom.

But if your primary desire is to feel safe, comfortable and unchallenged, you'll avoid asking the deeper questions that lead to the revelation of your true self.

So decide what you *know* you want most.

In regards to knowing, cats have a desire to know – and so do you.

Have you ever watched a cat enter a room it's not familiar with? It will sniff out all the different smells, find all the best hiding places (just in case) and listen to all the noises that arise, as if hearing them for the first time.

Each moment is new, and the cat knows this. It knows *this* sound is unique and not like the last sound. It knows that *this* smell is unique and not exactly like the last smell.

This is why it remains curious and open, rarely ever coming from memory or past. It makes no conclusions, because it knows this moment is the only reality. It knows that the only way to truly know something, it must not come from the past.

If you asked me what faculty you possess that would be the most useful in regard to waking up to what you are, I'd have to say – you guessed it – curiosity.

Curiosity is the innate desire to learn or discover something you don't yet know.

In our moment-to-moment existence, most of us don't question whether things are actually true or not. Most of us don't really take the time to investigate whether our beliefs, assumptions and ideas are actually so.

As a result, we suffer. In fact, unexamined beliefs are the number one reason we suffer.

Somehow we reason that belief is good enough. We forget that belief means that we really don't know – and we fool ourselves into thinking we do know.

But the thing is, we *can* know. We *can* realize what we really are. Despite what many traditions tell you, we don't have to stop short at belief. Belief isn't the last resort; there really is an alternative here. And this one has substance.

It is real knowing, the kind where doubt never arises anymore.

We don't intentionally engage in self-deception. It just happens. For the most part, we don't do much about it and we generally get the same results day after day. It simply becomes the way we live our lives, that is, until we get curious.

Sometimes it takes immense pain and suffering to make us curious. Sometimes it takes the death of a loved one to make us curious, and that's okay, so long as we begin to examine what we hold as true.

Until we begin to really examine what we hold as true, not much changes in our experience.

Deeply looking into what we assume as true is precisely what needs to happen if we truly desire to discover our true nature.

This discovery is beyond belief, conception, faith or dogma. Once made, you will never have any doubt about what you are again.

Be intensely curious about everything you automatically assume is true, because it is in this very investigation where your liberation awaits.

Unravel everything you've accumulated up to this point, and when the false is uprooted, only the truth remains.

What remains is what you ARE.

Like a cat, come from an open state of discovery, where this moment is the only reality, the 'last' moment is nothing but memory, and the 'next' moment is simply imagined.

Your orientation is everything, especially if you desire to see what you really are.

Curiosity didn't kill this cat (it woke him) ... and it certainly won't kill you.

Fear may arise, but so what. Fear is simply energy and it won't kill you, either.

With any luck at all, what *will* die is the belief in the person you thought you were, along with all of your false assumptions, ideas and cherished opinions. And in its place, the doubt-free realization of what you really are, what you've always been.

This is true freedom.

This is what you Are.

This is what you've always been.

But first, you must see through the 12 biggest obstacles to Enlightenment.

A whole lot of curiosity will be very useful in this quest.

Chapter 1
Lighten Up, Francis

The world is like a ride at an amusement park, and when you choose to go on it, you think it's real, because that's how powerful our minds are. And it's fun, for a while. Some people have been on the ride for a long time, and they begin to question: "Is this real, or is this just a ride?" And other people have remembered, and they come back to us and say, "Hey, don't worry, don't be afraid, ever, because this is just a ride!" AND WE KILL THOSE PEOPLE.

~ Bill Hicks (1961-1994)

Check out the above quote taken from a three and a half minute Youtube video of the late, irreverent comic named Bill Hicks. It's actually a great way to start reading this book. Simply Google the words, "Bill Hicks It's Just a Ride."

If those who recognize and remember say to us, "Hey, don't worry, it's just a ride" – and we sense they really *do* know, does it make any sense to be worried and afraid of this thing called enlightenment?

If those who recognize and remember who they really are come back and say, "Now I know why the Buddha was laughing! It really is ONE COSMIC JOKE", does it make any sense to approach this awakening business with a contracted, tense orientation?

Well, does it?

Do you think it's quite possible that you might have an underlying belief that says, "If I want anything worthwhile in life, then I must be serious about it?"

Being serious makes sense in a lot of cases, doesn't it?

In fact, in many cases, seriousness *is* required. Being serious is actually beneficial if what we want takes concerted effort over a period of time. Being serious is often practical and recommended in many instances.

But when it comes to waking up to what you already are, seeing what you have always been, a serious and tense approach doesn't really work best. In fact, it will often work against you.

The kind of seriousness that involves frustration, beating yourself up and wishing you were further along the path isn't very useful. But what about sincerity, you may ask? Yes, by all means. Be sincere. It goes a long way.

If awakening takes no effort and no time at all – a serious or heavy approach doesn't make much sense.

Granted, it takes a bit of looking and sustained attention, but that doesn't mean it takes contracted effort and struggle, does it?

Your true nature is always innately light and free, so arriving at it (or falling into it) with a heavy and encumbered attitude isn't the best way. For now, just take my word for it.

Just so you know, while reading this book, be aware that there is a conclusion-free zone (or dimension) that envelops you, watching you read this. You are the awareness that draws no conclusions at all. You are the aware, conclusion-free spaciousness that all conclusions arise in.

Seeing Through The 12 Biggest Obstacles To Enlightenment

Have you noticed that so many people find it very difficult to laugh at themselves? I mean, really laugh at themselves, the kind of hearty laugh that comes from the belly and not just the throat.

Why do we take ourselves so seriously? Why is it that we are quick to laugh at another's foibles, but not our own?

I'd have to say attachment to (and identification with) our ego prevents us from really being comfortable and secure in our own skin.

But let's get this out of the way right from the start. There is no ego. It's just a thought. There is no separate entity (called ego) to be found. Remove the label and it is simply the movement of thought.

I'm aware that there have been countless books written about it, and I know it's been the fall guy for a lot of unpleasant stuff, but it just doesn't exist. There is an idea called 'ego', but there is no actual ego to be found anywhere.

Look for it and see if you can find it.

And that's what the aim of this book is about: to see through the seeming obstacles that blind us in order to discover who we really are. Put simply, to dis-identify with the thinking mind as who we are, by recognizing the ever-present and undeniable presence of awareness that the thinking mind arises in.

Since so-called egos have a tendency to be fragile and in need of constant reinforcement, we generally don't like it when we're laughed at, or have become the butt of a joke.

We have no problem expressing (or playing to) our strengths, but when it comes to our weaknesses and so-called imperfections, we'd rather not have them out on full display for all to see.

If we liken ourselves to an artist holding an exhibit, we're much more likely to display all our great works for all to see, while leaving all of our "embarrassing," or "not-so great" works of art in the back room, with the door securely locked for none to see.

It is in denial and ignorance of our dual nature (as finite human beings) that we get caught between the infinite and the limited, the light and the dark, the good and the bad, the grandeur and the misery.

In truth, there is nothing embarrassing or imperfect about you. You are perfectly okay as you are.

Emptied of all notions, consider that all along you've been whole and complete, never lacking a thing. Consider the possibility who you really are has never been a limited, finite being with a certain life span, here to live for a while, only to die.

Those struggling with feeling good about who they are – warts and all – are operating under the illusion that they *should* be different than they are. And it's never true.

Granted, *you can* be different than you are, but not in this moment. You can only be as you already are in this moment. In another moment, you can be different, but not now, in this moment, the only reality there is.

We'd all be a lot happier if we just realized this.

In our ignorance and tendency to engage in self-deception, we deny our human dual nature, and place ourselves in a dis-ordered state of being. But in order to be a saint, one must first be a sinner. (They're both just concepts, by the way. There is no saint and there is no sinner.)

In order to be happy, one must first be sad. In order to be awake, one must first be asleep. In order to transcend the limits of our interpretations, one must first be trapped *in* those limits.

Wisdom sees the good sense of accepting who you are, right now – because if you don't, you further entrench what you don't want, thereby giving more life (energy) to what you don't want. This is called working against yourself. If we want peace and contentment in this life (and Self-discovery), we must naturally work with ourselves.

A preacher put this question to a class of children: *"If all the good people in the world were red and all the bad people were green, what color would you be?"* Little Jessica thought intensely for a moment and then her face lit up and she replied: *"Reverend, I'd be streaky!"*

That's real wisdom from a child unencumbered by the conditioned mind that judges, compares and condemns. All the while, what you really are simply watches, totally unharmed and totally welcoming.

Splitting our selves in two, we find ourselves in a constant daily battle. In an ongoing struggle to be something we're not, and to achieve something we think will make us "happy", we face the opposite direction of where peace and fulfillment is found.

Attempting to arrive at some place (other than where we presently are) guarantees discontent. Spending our attention and energy on trying to be the person others expect us to be guarantees discontent.

In the meantime, what is aware of all these movements to run from or please? Is this running away or trying to please?

It's your awareness, right? You know, that thing that never leaves, that's always there ... that thing we take for granted?

It seldom occurs to us to just stop and rest, and look at where we are, and consider that just maybe everything *is* okay as it is. Maybe it *is* perfectly fine as it is, and that a peaceful balance is only found by relaxing into our dual nature.

And just maybe there is something in us that is already deeply okay with everything as it is. What tells you that something isn't perfectly fine the way it is?

It's the mind that tells you something isn't perfectly fine as it is, right?

And you believe it.

But are you the mind?

Do you want the kind of peace that is unshakeable, the kind that doesn't depend on your mind's interpretations of things? Do you want the kind of peace that needs nothing in order to be at peace?

The peace that surpasses all understanding is not found in a peaceful mind. It is discovered in that which lies behind the mind. Your mind may be at peace, but it is not required in order for you to be at peace.

This book is about finding out what you really are, and what you really are is behind the mind. You are prior to the mind, you are beyond the mind, and you encompass the mind, simultaneously.

Use whichever pointer you like, or use them all. I use them all when pointing, but not necessarily at the same time. Whatever comes up in the moment is what I use.

Seeing the reality of our situation – that we can only live from our dual nature, and that we already are living *from* our dual nature, we can relax in that knowing – and notice what arises.

If we chase after or strive for happiness, while suppressing our unhappiness, happiness will elude us.

The paradox of happiness dictates that when we align ourselves with truth and not falsehood – and stop arguing with reality – our natural state of happiness can't help *but* arise.

To be wholly unconcerned, yet intimately engaged, it is requisite that we live our lives engaged in whatever life is moving us to do, without concern whether we're doing it 'right', or performing to our 'best' ability.

Since there are no mistakes, our peace and security lies in knowing we can't do it "wrong". In fact, there's no such thing as "doing it wrong." To be wholly unconcerned and intimately engaged means that we aren't preoccupied with how we're being perceived, what it looks like, or how it will turn out.

So Relax.

Being detached from our interpretations and meanings of things, we transfer all that energy towards just showing up fully, without insisting our agenda be met.

There are no mistakes.

Wisdom sees that unhappiness arises when we don't want what we have, and happiness arises when we want what we have. How simple.

When we look at the beauty of say, a waterfall cascading down a lush gorge, or a majestic mountain peak covered in snow, with the setting sun just beyond it, our breath is taken away. At first sight of this scenery, we have a tendency to gasp in awe.

All other activity is suspended and we're simply aware, noticing our desire to take in what we see. In this seeing, we find ourselves resting in the beauty of the scene, and we never want it to end.

We don't want anything *from* our object of affection; we find ourselves in deep gratitude just for the ability to witness it. In this witnessing, all grasping and moving-away tendencies spontaneously dissolve, and we are left relaxing into our basic and fundamental awareness.

This fundamental awareness is what you are.

Resting with the world, without any desire to change or fix it, all is perfect as it is. Awareness doesn't care how it unfolds. It's just aware.

Much like grace, nature has a way of grabbing us against our will, thus suspending our will. Ushered into a quiet clear space, we are emptied of desire, agitation and self-contraction.

And in this space, where time is no longer sensed, we sense oneness with everything, without any boundary between our selves and what we see. The two are one – and there's no denying this.

In this quiet, open space where time is suspended, we find ourselves aware and totally present. In that moment, subtle revelations, deeper insights and flashes of higher truths may be revealed to us, stoking a fire inside that burns away anything unlike it.

Temporarily transported from our daily lives, we revel in the magnificence of the scenery that removes any desire or need to have it any other way than it is.

In fact, we are given a glimpse into what it's like to live in the timeless now, where no problems exist – where everything simply arises perfectly and completely, as it is.

It is in this calm moment of being in the eye of the storm where we realize that it is our mind that erects barriers, and judges what arises as good or bad, right or wrong.

Without referring to thought to tell us about a thing, we see absolutely everything as already perfect the way it is.

Nature reminds us, not so much by its scenery, but what it does *to* us and what it does *in* us: it steals our desire to be elsewhere. This isn't merely an exercise in imagination; this is the real thing.

This beauty pervades everything in the cosmos and it is only the mind that tells us a different story, a story based on what the five, limited sensory tools perceive. Believing what our five senses tell us, we believe that perception is reality.

And we suffer.

It's like expecting an unawake man to explain the awakened perspective, or waiting for a severely drunken man not to slur. No matter what explanation is given, it will never match reality.

But what might happen if we could see the entire universe (and everything in it) as being utterly beautiful, like the exquisite scene in nature that suspends our will? What if we saw that every single arising, as it is, without exception, *as* an object of immense beauty?

It was seen because we were light and free, empty of the seriousness that would prevent that seeing.

Just as the extraordinarily beautiful object in nature suspends our will, so too, would the contemplation of everything ordinary in the universe *as* an object of beauty would open our awareness to the truth that whatever arises *is* as it should be, without exception.

All of our running towards pleasure and away from pain would immediately come to rest – and through grace, our self-contraction lifted. We discover that we naturally embrace *all* that we are, freely.

What a contrast from the way most humans resist going into that good night, raging against the dying of the light! While pain and pleasure most certainly appear in nature, they never become problems to be taken seriously.

Dogs wag their tails in excitement when asked to go for a ride in the car, or for a walk in the park. When it experiences pain, it yelps. When not in any pain, it's not concerned about it, nor is it worried that it may come back later.

It doesn't dread future pain and doesn't hold on to past pain. It's all a very natural and simple affair. We may say nature is just ignorant and doesn't know any better, but nature is far more intelligent than we'll ever be.

Nature is not only smarter than we think – nature is smarter than we *can* think.

While many humans puff out their chests proclaiming to be the most intelligent species in the entire universe, nature humbly sits back and chuckles, knowing it produced the mind that claims that.

Nature is label-free, forever lacking any desire to classify and discern all the numerous forms it displays. It doesn't need to say, "These animals look different from those animals, so let's call these animals *tigers* and these animals *giraffes*."

Or, "Hurricanes are bad and do so much damage, but light rain showers are good for the growth of vegetables and flowers, so embracing light showers while resisting hurricanes is wise."

No labels, no problems. No boundaries, no problems. No story, no suffering. Absolutely everything arises from the same singular source and is independent of any story or feeling about it.

Like nature, wanting absolutely nothing other than what actually arises, and wanting nothing other than what you are – as you are – you are timelessly frozen in paralysis by the sheer beauty and perfection that shows up all around you.

Being released from past clinging to misguided notions, you are freshly undone as one who made distinctions, however small. As Meister Eckhart said, *"To have that consciousness where distinction never gazed"* is what you're operating from.

"Being in the world, but not of it," Jesus said.

And nothing is left out. Not a single particle of dust is excluded from this beauty, no matter how "unsightly," "scary" or "untimely."

You see it radiating from every object of your affection, and simultaneously, that same beauty radiates from within you, out to the world. No longer believing in the existence of boundaries, separation and division fall away.

All because you weren't so judgmental and serious.

Free of pride and full of gratitude and authentic humility, you can't help *but* see perfection all around you. In that seeing, you know you *never* had imperfections – you just believed you did, because you were taught to believe you did.

Embracing who you are *as* you are, you watch guilt, shame and remorse drop away. And with it, hope and fear, too. Who needs hope for a better tomorrow when it's always right now?

Who needs hope when you accept what is, as is?

Who needs to seek anymore when it is finally seen that what you were looking for is doing the looking?

Since fear is born of separation, who invites fear when there is no separation? Who invites fear when it is realized that nothing external *can* cause our experience of fear?

The source of our angst and anxiety was our habitual inclination to view the opposites as never coming together, never arising in unison.

We believed they were divorced from each other, like two good people from a bad marriage. Most of our problems came from believing that the opposites can and should be separated from one another.

Most of our shame and insecurity came from resisting or running from the "bad" half, the side we deemed "imperfect" and "flawed."

Realizing that all opposites are actually aspects of one underlying reality, we see through the illusion of imperfection and perfection, and free ourselves from the pairs of opposites.

Consequently, we are liberated from the nonsensical challenges involved in the war of opposites.

No longer do we try to hide from (or compensate for) what we may still perceive as the "less than ideal" side of our abilities and characteristics. Dropping that heavy burden we carried for so long, we can't help but notice how much lighter our load is.

Recognizing that the point was never to pit one side against the other in search of peace, we unify and harmonize the polarities by discovering the ground that encompasses both.

Resting in this ground that includes both the "positive and negative" aspects, we transcend both.

But, we may ask, if we see the moment as it is without any need to alter or fix it – and if we see all of ourselves as we ARE, without any need to hide or compensate for, will we lose our drive in the name of improvement?

What will happen to us if we see our opposites as one? What will happen if we become actually grateful for our so-called imperfections and see them in an entirely new light?

What if we finally recognize, that without our "less than ideal" half, we couldn't experience who we are, let alone experience anything at all? What might happen if we see the conditions of existence as mutually interdependent upon each other, as the quantum physicists have already proven?

If we're fortunate, we'll lose our misperception that our happiness depends on accepting our strengths, while resisting our weaknesses.

When the opposites of all of our characteristics and traits are seen as one – and *already* in harmony – already and always a beautiful melody of comfort and discomfort, pleasure and pain, insecure and secure, then our old battles and enemies become dances and lovers.

When we empty ourselves of all our notions and opinions, we are left with the fullness and completeness of life – all in perfect harmony. Then, and only, then, are we in a position to make friends with ALL of it, not just half of it.

Then, and only, then, do we give ourselves the opportunity to notice what we are, what we've always been – the silent, awake space of awareness that freely gives rise to all of it – even the seriousness.

Right where you are is exactly where you are meant to be.

Only a thought will tell you different.

So lighten up, Francis.

See that wishing you were "further along the path" is counterproductive and time-bound.

Abandon yourself to what is. Complete abandonment to You as you are – to This, as it is, Right Now, is the way through.

As soon as you allow yourself to be imprisoned to whatever binds you right now, at that very instant, you are no longer imprisoned.

Be deluded unreservedly and it transforms to wisdom, or fall back into the familiar pattern and resist and suffer.

See that there is nothing you must do or attain in order to be what you already are.

And then, upon SEEING THIS, if you feel compelled, be a light unto another and point the way.

But first, be a light unto yourself.

There's no greater service you can render the world.

There's nothing more rewarding.

From someone who rarely makes promises, that's a promise.

Chapter 2
The Devil You Know

We have names for everything. What if we forgot about those names? And we stopped seeing things as something? What if we just observed things, watched things, without giving them a name, without coming to a conclusion? What do you think would happen? You would transcend everything.

~ Robert Adams

    The primary function of the mind is to know what is going on at all times, in order to remain safe, secure and in control.

    Have you noticed?

    You are not the mind – the activity of thinking that endlessly attempts to 'know' everything as it arises.

    If you think you are the mind, as the mind goes, you go.

    You are not the body either.

    If you are not the mind or the body, then what is left?

    You are the pure awareness that the mind and body appear in.

    Mind (not You) compares, analyzes and evaluates what is

presently happening against its database of stored knowledge, so it can come up with an appropriate response.

It generally doesn't like surprises and doesn't like to be caught off guard.

Control and survival are its two primary desires, and when that is threatened in any way, the mind kicks into high gear, efficiently referencing what it *thinks* it knows in order to remain safe and secure.

Like pushing 'enter' after you just punched in your Google search term, the mind quickly retrieves the appropriate response.

In its infinite wisdom, it thinks what it knows is ultimately more valuable than what it doesn't know.

It actually believes it can approach the unknown with the known. It will continue with this approach until it exhausts itself. Then it tries some more.

Most people would rather spend time with the devil they know instead of the devil they don't know.

At least they're comfortable, even if they're uncomfortable. It is familiar, and the mind loves familiar.

Children will cling to the severely abusive parents they know rather than moving towards the loving, foster parents they don't know. It's just how we're wired.

More accurately, it's how the identified mind is wired.

If we have any purpose at all in life, it is to dis-identify with the mind and awaken to our Real Identity.

We are creatures of habit, with a strong tendency to remain with the known, even if the known continues to prove disadvantageous and hurtful.

If we intuitively know our freedom lies in the unknown, why do we insist on clinging to the known?

Seeing Through The 12 Biggest Obstacles To Enlightenment

How has this strategy worked so far? Has everything you've come to know and believe delivered what you really want?

Wisdom blooms when you see that none of your "knowledge" has brought you to the realization that you are the Impersonal One that is doing the looking.

What you "know" has not brought you relief from the pain and suffering that continues to weaken your energy because of your belief in who you think you are.

What do you really want? Have you ever really identified this?

Is feeling comfortable and safe the most important thing?

What are you willing to endure to get what you really want?

If you look and see in your direct experience that what you cling to you are bound by, you might reconsider the value of clinging to the known.

Aren't you bound by your self-image, your opinion of yourself, and your opinion of others – good, bad or indifferent?

Take solace in the fact that "you" aren't doing it.

The mind is.

Are you the mind? No, You aren't.

You are the silent, witnessing, aware presence that is prior to the mind, untouched and unharmed by the contents of the mind.

Don't believe this. See this in your direct experience. It's simple.

Some call this Spirit or Awareness, but it really doesn't matter what you call it because the word and what you call it is never the actual.

When this truth goes from belief that resides above the neck, to realization below the neck, the clinging to the known will cease automatically.

Truth really does set you free.

So you don't have to try and stop clinging to the known.

Rather, see what you really are and the rest will take care of itself, all by itself.

Promise.

Resting in the unknown will come naturally – after You see.

You don't have to hope, as all hope will vanish with seeing.

Hope for something other than what you already have and wishing for a particular future dissolves in the knowing that there is only this timeless moment as it is.

Who needs hope when everything is perfectly okay as it is?

Fear dissolves in the knowing of what you really are, never in the belief or assumption of who you think you are.

Who creates fear when it is finally known there is nothing *to* fear?

Fear arises for the one who still believes they are a separate entity among many other separate entities.

Do you think fear arises for the One who knows it's all One, for the One who knows there is no other?

Do you think fear arises when it is known that it's all a defense against nothing?

There is ONE BEING in many forms.

There is ONE ANIMATING POWER that informs everything.

There is only ONE thing going on, without separation or division. It is both source and substance.

Knowing this, we no longer project ourselves backward in guilt and forward in anxiety – and we let our fictions end, every single one of them.

In place of our stories and fictions about existence, we live authentically in an open state of discovery, aware when we attempt to delude ourselves.

We don't condemn and beat ourselves up anymore because we know that whatever unfolds couldn't have unfolded any different.

When the mind says otherwise, we smile and don't believe a word of it.

Besides, there is no "me" it happens to.

No longer do we look to any outside agency to tell us what is real and true.

We know it's all an inside game, always and in all ways.

No longer do we deceive ourselves about our responsibility for our own experience.

We know we're responsible for all of it, impersonally.

Deceiving ourselves about the richness and beauty of life, as it is, just isn't possible anymore.

In this quiet, open space of discovery where time is suspended, it is discovered that aware presence is all there is. Everything comes from that, is made of that and returns to that.

In that moment, subtle revelations, deeper insights and flashes of higher truths may be revealed to us, stoking a fire inside that burns away anything and everything unlike it.

We are given a glimpse of what it is like to live in the timeless now, where absolutely no problems exist, where nothing is known but what you are.

Seeing Through The 12 Biggest Obstacles To Enlightenment

Where everything simply arises, perfectly and completely.

If this moment is fresh and new, how can anything truly be known about it?

Wisdom is in the knowing that you don't know.

No amount of thinking, no matter how "deep" and insightful, can ever tell you what you are. What you are is beyond conception. What you are is the non-conceptual awareness that thinking arises from.

Whoever you think you are, that's not it. It's entirely something else. And that 'something else' can never be adequately described because it is beyond description. However, THIS THAT YOU ARE can be pointed to.

So when you look in the direction in which you are being pointed to (using concepts), resist the temptation to try to mentally comprehend the words and assign meaning to them. You won't ever understand this.

On one particular day, a bull strayed into the forest. He came upon green grass and began to graze. He continued on deeper and deeper into the forest. After a few weeks of being deep in the forest, he grew lazy and fat – all food and no work.

Then one day, an old lion well beyond his years and having difficulty hunting prey, stumbled upon this fat bull. He couldn't believe his luck. Easier to stalk and kill a bull than a deer he thought.

Patiently, the lion waited for the right time and pounced on the bull, killing him and eating him up. His stomach become very full and he roared in great contentment.

It just so happened that there was a hunter nearby who heard the roar, tracked down the lion and shot him dead.

The moral of the story: When you're so full of bull, you should not open your mouth!

When we empty ourselves of all our notions, assumptions and opinions, we are left with the fullness and completeness of life, as it is.

Then, and only then, are we able to make room for something of a higher order to move through us, like the knowing-realization that you are life itself, simultaneously the source, substance and appearance of all.

Only when the mind doesn't know can the Sacred Flower Bloom into Consciousness.

Let go of who you *think* you are for the opportunity to realize what you are.

Resist the urge to fall into the trap of hanging out with the devil you know, instead of the devil you don't know.

Because I can tell you, there is only the constant and unknowable wonder of being.

Only when you begin to see that all of your accumulated knowledge hasn't gotten you anywhere, can a whole new potential arise.

The One is wisdom while who you think you are looks to become wise.

The One is knowledge while who you think you are looks to become knowledgeable.

Only when we allow ourselves NOT to know do we give ourselves the opportunity *to* know.

In the end, or rather, right from the beginning, there is something in you knowing the thoughts, feelings, perceptions and sensations. This awareness is illuminating or knowing all these things that appear in it.

Your true nature is that which knows all these appearances. It is nothing more than the sense of knowingness that is within you now.

Seeing Through The 12 Biggest Obstacles To Enlightenment

It is the one thing you cannot deny, that fact that you exist and are aware.

Because it is assumed to be complex and involved, it is overlooked for an entire lifetime by most. But it's okay; nobody is keeping score.

Awareness is ever-present and seen clearly. Simply by asking, "What is knowing thoughts, and what is knowing the lack of thoughts?" points you back to what you are.

You need nothing to be what you are, so simply rest in what you are.

Your own sense of existence-awareness is immediately known and available all the time.

See without any confusion at all that you are the presence of awareness that is always and fundamentally at the basis of everything experienced.

And be done with both devils!

Chapter 3
Dancing With The Dead

Said a traveler to one of the disciples, "I have traveled a great distance to listen to the Master, but I find his words quite ordinary." "Don't listen to his words, listen to his message." "How does one do that?" "Take hold of a sentence that he says, shake it well till all the words drop off. What is left will set your heart on fire."

~ Anthony deMello

Have you considered just how much thought (thinking) causes so much suffering, not only in your own life, but in the life of every human being?

I am sure we could all agree that it is immense.

And the interesting part is that something that isn't even alive is the cause of all this suffering!

All thought (thinking) is past.

Therefore, all thinking is dead.

Yet we continually attempt to resurrect what is already and completely dead.

Not only can't you find or locate thought, when it arises, it's already gone.

I remember when I first came across this pointer that all thought is past.

It fascinated me, and since I knew it was a huge, transforming insight, I was determined to see if it was true or not.

Sure enough, as soon as thought arises, whoosh, it was gone, in and out of awareness in a nanosecond.

I was actually surprised I hadn't seen it sooner. It was simple to notice. To be more accurate with words, there was surprise it wasn't seen sooner. (There was no "I" that saw it. It was seen).

Then I saw the habit of the mind to try to latch onto thought, especially if it was a pleasant thought – and the habit of the mind to try to run from thought, especially if it was an unpleasant thought.

This clinging or avoiding was the mechanism that kept me on the wheel of suffering.

There is no technique or trick to end suffering. See through the false idea that there is an "I" who can suffer, and suffering dies off.

When it was seen (by no one) that all thought is indeed past, something let go.

I am prior to the mind; I am free of the thoughts of the mind. Whatever the mind says about me is ultimately untrue.

What I am, the Radiant Light of Awareness that illumines all, is utterly unaffected by absolutely everything, including any thought or emotion, pleasant or unpleasant.

When it was seen that there was no "me", a separate entity believed to be the author of thought, something let go.

You could call it a radical release, and immediately I felt lighter and freer.

Once you have broken through the belief in the reality of thought and see it for what it is, there is no going back to identifying with the thinking mind as who you are.

Thoughts still arise, but now you know they arise in the untouched, space of thought-free awareness you are.

Do not argue or go to war with thoughts. It only gives more life to them. Instead, watch them float by and dissipate in the awareness you are.

Does the presence of clouds ever touch the sun? Does thought and emotion, no matter how intense, ever block the fact of your own being-awareness?

If you give all your attention and reality to the clouds, you will forever be stuck *in* the clouds. Place your attention on the Real Source, the awareness that gives rise to thoughts, and clouds will never bother you again.

Shift the focus to that which is already free of thought and emotion – and notice the peace that comes with that.

For you to have a problem, thought must arise.

See this.

As Bob Adamson likes to say, "What's wrong with right now unless you think about it?"

Thought is your only problem. More accurately, belief in thought is your only problem.

Believing the thoughts are yours is the main culprit.

The solution is to question the mind itself, not to solve its questions.

Since there is no becoming in being, you don't one day become free. Rather, through a deep investigation, you notice your present freedom, that which needs nothing in order to *be* free.

Again, this is all about noticing what is <u>already</u> the case...

It's a peeling away process – an unlearning process – so throw away ALL your conceptions, every last one of them!

Thought suddenly becomes totally and absolutely irrelevant. It is noticed that no thought can touch what you really are. Thoughts come and go in what you are, and can never *be* what you are.

See this for yourself right now, in your own direct experience, and be free from the identification *with* thoughts!

If what you are is the non-conceptual space of awake, aware presence that cannot be comprehended, see the folly of identifying with any word or thought that attempts to accurately describe what you are.

You are the non-conceptual presence of awareness that thinking arises in. Realizing what you are cannot be approached with thought.

This reminds me of a Zen parable: *"What, concretely, is Enlightenment?" "Seeing Reality as it is," said the Master. "Doesn't everyone see Reality as it is?" "Oh, no!* **Most people see it as they think it is.*" "What's the difference?" "The difference between thinking you are drowning in a stormy sea and knowing you cannot drown because there isn't any water in sight for miles around."*

How can the finite mind ever comprehend the infinite?

Prior to thinking that comes and goes, and prior to the mind that will one day die, You are the No-thing, the eternal and ever-present awake awareness that those 'things' arise and set in.

When it was seen that thinking happens on its own, without me, things started to really cook.

Seeing that I wasn't the author of thinking, that I didn't

decide to think (and that thinking happens all by itself), was a huge turning point.

For almost 40 years, I thought I was the one doing the thinking.

And I wondered why it was so hard to change my thoughts!

I thought I was actually deciding to think certain thoughts, including the miserable and self-defeating ones that made it difficult for you to be around me.

But if I chose my thoughts, why would I ever choose an unhappy thought?

If I chose my thoughts, why couldn't I always think pleasant, uplifting thoughts?

See through the illusion that you are thinking thoughts and be free.

Since birth, it has been drilled into us that there is a past and a future – and that we can make our life work by learning from our past and preparing for our future. Neither has any reality except in our mind.

If the so-called mind that comes and goes isn't innately real, how can what it produces (and believes in) be real, or deliver the Real?

Since most of us believe the thoughts in our head, we feel guilt and shame about the thoughts we think. Since most of us believe the thoughts in our head, we feel guilt and shame about our past, and fear and anxiety about our future.

This is the inevitable consequence of identification with the mind that believes in a past and a future, with the mind that constructs a past and a future.

To be awake and free is to see that this moment is all there is, and that anything else is created and sustained by the mind.

To be awake and free is to see that if it doesn't pertain to *this* time-less moment, it is dead.

To be awake and free means you know that time is a mental construct. You know that you keep the past, a dead thing, alive with memory. You know that you keep the future, a dead thing, alive with anticipation and imagination.

Without referring to thought, is there a past or future? Without referring to thought, can you have a problem?

Don't gloss over this. It is essential. Look and really see.

You'll see, on present evidence, that there is no past or future unless you think about it.

In other words, for a problem to exist, thought must arise.

No thought, no problem.

If you are depressed, you are living in the past – a dead thing.

If you are anxious, you are living in the future – an imagined thing.

If you are at peace, you are living in the present – the only thing.

But as we've already seen, there isn't a "you" that lives in a present moment. Even if we always fail, we still have to use words in our attempts to describe the indescribable.

If we aren't awake to what is real and true, we live our lives from the filter of the past, and from the filter of a future. In other words, we live from the mind that creates time.

And since we have a strong sense of having a past, we conclude that there must *be* a past. But what is it that convinces us of a past?

It is memory and it is memory alone.

While we see that in our direct experience there is only an endless present, without beginning, middle or end, there is something that speaks quite clearly and vehemently of things that were – of things that happened moments ago, days ago, months ago, and years ago.

Again, it is memory.

And while we cannot see the past, feel the past or touch the past, we can surely (and quite vividly) remember the past. But we can only ever do this presently, in the present moment.

We somehow make the leap and think that memory provides us actual knowledge of an actual past, even if we can't directly experience any *actual* past.

However, memory is always a present experience, is it not?

We can only know the past in the present, and as part of the present only.

Wisdom sees that time is mind, and that time equals suffering. We can't possibly suffer if we stay in this present moment, where this is no time.

No time + no thought believed in = peace.

When we no longer reference the past as something real and true, we live in the one, true reality. In fact, You already do.

This is the kingdom of heaven Jesus spoke of, and it is no further than right where you are, now and always. And it's always now.

This eternal and timeless moment doesn't come and go. It is the one constant, and everything else comes and goes in it.

All is transient and impermanent, while You ARE the eternal now.

See the unreality of the past.

See the false as false and be free.

Self-realization only happens in the immediacy of this moment. Fresh and new is only found now, not in the imagined future, and certainly not in the memory of past.

Now that you are reading this sentence, the one prior you just read is stale, without any aliveness to it.

If you access memory and thought to tell you what is true, you access a dead thing.

Anything we bring from the past is a dead thing that we give life to. Past, being memory only, is a dead thing. So don't look for truth there.

Mind is thought and thought can't recognize this. The kind of seeing we're talking about here has nothing to do with the intellect or mind.

Pure, conscious awareness, that which is devoid of that, is completely unrelated to thought. If there is any relation at all, it is that mind and thought arise in awareness, and is not independent *of* awareness.

In other words, without awareness, thought can't be.

Living reality is only discovered in this present moment, not the prior moment or the next one, but in this eternal, timeless moment.

Because our attention is life giving and supportive, what we give our attention and belief to lives on and shapes our experience.

When we cling to and insist on a belief that says, "This is what enlightenment looks like," we put on life support that which is already dead.

Get a living will and sign it now! Don't put on life support (and prolong) that which is already dead.

We resurrect what was already dead, and carry around our propped up version of truth, hoping it stands up.

Seeing Through The 12 Biggest Obstacles To Enlightenment

We prop it up as real and alive, just like the dead guy in "Weekend at Bernie's." As much as we try to present the picture of aliveness, it's dead through and through.

Then, we live from that lie believed in – and illusion and confusion ensues. If our foundation is built on illusion, we know what happens when the first storm rolls in.

It doesn't stand up. It washes away, because our foundation was never rooted in what is sustainable and real.

Self-deception rooted in illusion is painful, but telling the truth isn't.

Telling the truth may be scary at first, and it may be painful at first, but in the end, the rewards far outweigh any difficulty experienced in the beginning.

Awaken from the idea of a past, from the idea of a future.

And stop dancing with the dead.

Seeing what you really are depends on it.

Remember, mind lives in time.

YOU don't.

Chapter 4
Seek And Don't Find

We are so engrossed with the objects, or appearances revealed by the light, that we pay no attention to the light.

~ Ramana Maharshi

You may have come across the statement "seek and don't find."

And that seeking implies that you are reinforcing the idea that there is a separate someone who needs to find out what they are – all the while fully being what they are, already fully being what they seek.

The implication is that seeking is a problem, and that it perpetuates the idea that the very act of seeking presupposes that there is a seeker in the first place. I don't view it that way.

Besides, this realization doesn't happen until after clearly seeing there is no one home.

If I didn't continue to look at everything I held as true, regardless of whether I was expecting to find anything, I am not so sure that the onion would have been peeled away to the final layer-less layer.

I had to peel, I had to seek, in order to discover that upon peeling all the layers away, nothing was left at the end. This nothing, it was discovered, is what I AM.

In truth, "I" wasn't doing the seeking because there never was an "I" that did the looking. Looking and seeking was being done, but by no one.

Consciousness was seeking.

The act of seeing, looking and investigating was never done by "me" – and certainly not by any separate entity that can be found.

I've never done anything.

I am not the doer. I've never been the doer of anything.

Things are done, but a doer cannot be found.

Thinking I was the doer caused so much suffering – and for so many years!

When we seek for something, we expect to find something, don't we?

We think we'll find something out in front of us.

We reason that if we don't have it now, we must go in search of it in order to get it.

We go on a journey in time looking to find what we are.

We innocently assume we can find what we're looking for. Otherwise, why would we bother looking?

We think we'll find an object, because we unconsciously assume that indeed, we are the subject that can find an object.

But hold up.

You can't find what you already are.

And there isn't a "you" that can find anything, including who you think you are.

That's just more dualism.

If you could find what you already are, you would have to be an object.

You are not an object.

"God" can never be an object of its own knowledge, just as a knife can't cut itself, just as fire can't burn itself, and just as light can't illuminate itself.

If you are not an object, you must be the subject.

Truth can never be found, because truth isn't an object to *be* found.

How can you find the Finder?

Can the eye see itself?

Can you find you?

Can a 'no you' find a "you"?

See there is no "you" and all this will be resolved.

See through the illusion of the separate self and all your troubles will melt away.

When seeking, the mind has all kinds of imaginings and none of them are especially useful. They all take the focus off what is most revealing, and that is what is eternally present and clear within.

If we get this, we get everything that matters.

If this is seen, dis-identification with the thinking mind as who we are is imminent.

One of those imaginings is that the understanding of what we are is an experience, but it can't be that because all experience has a certain life span. All life spans arise and set in what you are, the unborn, the undying.

You don't feel awareness. Awareness, what you are, is

not a feeling. All feelings come and go and therefore, can't be what you are. Feelings come and go in the constant awareness you are. While awareness appears to ebb and flow, it does not.

You cannot lose what is eternally present.

What in you right now is present and aware?

Does this ever come and go? Is this presence or awareness ever clouded over? Even in your darkest hours, what you are shines brightly, never leaving you.

Awareness comes with no bells and whistles that the mind prefers.

The presence of awareness is so subtle it's overlooked. The mind isn't tuned into the subtle. Rather, it looks for the outrageous, the obvious, and that which is remarkable and worth commenting on.

Our entire mental functioning is designed towards seeking something external, something we can pinpoint and name.

However, what we are isn't something external that can be found. What we are can't be grasped with thought.

It's just here, without any fanfare, or need to take credit for anything.

It never jumps out at you saying, "Here I am!"

It makes no demand to be seen, and yet, it is the reason anything is seen and perceived.

It is the silent background where all activity and noise appears in.

It is the unknown formless container in which all form is known.

It is the subtle space of emptiness where the not-so-

Seeing Through The 12 Biggest Obstacles To Enlightenment

subtle world of form and things manifest.

You are this subtle awareness!

Without the exclamation point, that is.

Seek and don't find.

However, while you won't find anything, the good news is that what is discovered is that what you are looking for is what is looking.

Like light, it cannot itself be seen, yet it illuminates all that is seen.

Who needs to seek anymore when it is finally discovered that what you are looking for is what is looking?

And when *that* is discovered (by no one) resist the urge to take on a new identity and erect another barrier that says, "Ah, this is who I am! I am the witnessing awareness, the watcher of all."

But where is this watcher located?

Wouldn't that imply a separate entity?

Can you find it?

Tell the truth.

What is watching the watcher?

Can that be seen?

Thinking you can find what you REALLY ARE is a big obstacle to enlightenment.

Bring your best shovel.

You'll be digging all the way to China.

It will forever have you looking 'out there' for something that inherently can never *be* found out there.

There isn't an "out there."

Seeing Through The 12 Biggest Obstacles To Enlightenment

There is just this and nothing else – no direction, no boundary, and no opposition.

To enjoy the spectacular view, stop looking East if you want to enjoy the setting sun.

Chapter 5
No Path To Now

We suffer from a hallucination, from a false and distorted sensation of our own existence as living organisms. Most of us have the sense that "I myself" is a separate center of feeling and action, living inside and bounded by the physical body – a center which 'confronts' an 'external' world of people and things, making contact through the sense with a universe both alien and strange.

~ Alan Watts

It is worth repeating: The mind lives in time, YOU don't.

Since mind works in time, it will never apprehend the timeless.

If you think you ARE the mind, you will continue to live in imagined time, complete with fear, insecurity and suffering.

Time plays out on a conceptual level and depends on thinking.

Being does not.

Granted, time has its place in practical affairs, but when this carries over into the realm of knowing your real nature, the concept of time is entirely empty of any useful value.

If you know your real nature as the silent, aware and awake presence that is behind the mind and outside of time, you live in this, the eternal and timeless now.

No longer do you reference the so-called past to tell you what is so.

Pain can arise, but it's not resisted, so it doesn't hang around. It moves through, like dark clouds on a clear, sunny sky.

If you can perceive pain, how can you *be* the pain? You can't be what you perceive, can you?

So much of what has been conveyed throughout the ages (and what will continue to be conveyed) is that in order to awaken to your true nature, you must go on a journey – and a spiritual one at that!

The message is that you, too, must walk that well-trodden path.

The typical paths are still subtly holding out a better future, a freer, more enlightened state in the future. The problem is, is that time is a mental construct, so there is no freedom or better state in a non-existent reality.

We believe in the journey. What solidifies this belief is that many things in life require a journey (a process in time and a maturing in time), in order to achieve the goal we set out to achieve.

So why would this enlightenment business be any different?

Assuming it *isn't* any different, we hunker down and commit to the journey, no matter how long it takes.

Contributing to this assumption that it takes time and effort to wake up is our nagging bouts of low self-esteem, our insecurities, and our yearning to feel whole and complete.

We may even think we don't have what it takes, that we

haven't earned it, or that we aren't spiritual enough, wise enough, or even special and worthy enough.

We assume, as we are right now, we don't have or possess what is needed to awaken. We may even think it's for the chosen few and that it is indeed, rare.

Because we don't measure up, we need to improve ourselves if we want to attain enlightenment and see as the enlightened see.

We reason that we're obviously missing something essential, or we wouldn't be feeling the way we feel!

And it's all baloney, every last bit of it.

We think it's about addition, when in fact it is all about subtraction. It's a tearing down process, not a building up process.

There is no development or deepening in what you already are. If you really are utterly and absolutely perfect and free right now (You Are), it hardly makes any sense that you need to develop or deepen anything.

The whole notion of deepening implies time, and that you have a problem that needs time to fix.

It implies that you aren't already deep enough, complete enough or whole enough as you are.

None of the great non-dual traditions have ever communicated that you need to become something other than what you already are, or get to anything (or anywhere) other than where you already are.

Unfortunately, many seekers are still attempting to develop, purify and deepen their experience – and years later they're still doing the same thing, not realizing they have everything they need.

We are, as we are, more than enough, right now. And it's a simple matter of recognition, not of deepening or improving what you are.

We are, as we are, fully capable of discovering what we really are, in this timeless moment.

Not next month, next year, or after you've meditated for five years, but this moment.

And it's always this moment. There isn't a next moment, nor is there a moment that just passed.

All arises and fades in this, eternal moment.

There is literally nothing you need to become in order to see this. This is about being, not becoming.

There is no becoming in being. There never was.

There is no progression in the Ground of Being.

There is no path to now.

Drop the idea that you need more time to get this; it's just another idea arising in time-less Being.

No journey is needed, so put down your backpack and lighten your load.

There is no more anxiety or progression, steps or stages for an individual that never was in the first place.

The unkempt, homeless man who scours trash cans looking for food and the selfless woman who tirelessly manages two, non-profit charity organizations that benefit thousands are both equally worthy of seeing this.

There is no outside higher agency that withholds or bestows self-realization based on behavior.

Journeys imply time when there is none – and time is mind.

You're after the time-less... that which never enters the stream of imagined time.

And the time-less can never be approached via time or the mind, which are essentially one and the same.

There is only this; there is only what is happening, all within what you are. You are the ever-present space that equally allows absolutely everything to come and go in.

Absolutely nothing is outside of what you are. Absolutely nothing is separate from what you are.

You aren't living in this world; the world is within you.

All is one and You ARE THAT ONE.

And so, the popular teaching that says you must journey in time in order to discover what you are is not only an obstacle to the realization of what you are, it's a great way to delay the discovery of what you are.

And trust me, the mind wants this delay. In fact, it creates this delay.

The mind deals in appearances, and never reality. To know the real, you must look beyond the mind to the knowing principle that illuminates the mind.

The mind, being an appearance within the manifestation, can never get this. This is about looking into the source *of* the appearance. The mind will never understand what is beyond the mind.

The idea of a journey sets up in the mind that a long and arduous search filled with meditation, breathing exercises, mantras, devotion, etc. is needed for the seeker.

And so, off on a journey it goes.

There is nothing to attain or practice. All practices are at the level of the mind. There is no path to navigate to take you to your own being.

Seeing what is already so takes literally no time at all. No effort, strife and struggle, either.

Seeing Through The 12 Biggest Obstacles To Enlightenment

You don't need a single thing to be what you are.

Drop the notion that techniques and answers are required to exist and be aware. You don't need any technique or answer to know who you are without any doubt.

The simple realization of who you are is directly perceived prior to conceptual activity, right now.

Even a lazy man can see this.

Chapter 6
Ignoring Direct Experience

When you can see everything as it is, you will also see yourself as you are. It is like cleaning a mirror. The same mirror that shows you the world as it is will also show you your own face. The thought, "I am" is the polishing cloth. Use it.

~ Nisargadatta Maharaj

When we are ignorant of anything, essentially we *ignore* what is true. Ignore what is true, and suffer the consequences that generally follow.

Anytime we act out of ignorance, we're naturally suppressing wisdom. Anytime we act from wisdom, we naturally suppress ignorance.

Ignorant of truth, we turn away from what is true and invariably suffer from illusion. Illusion generally hurts. It's not personal; it's just the way it works.

Have you noticed?

Paying attention to what is true (what doesn't come and go; what is always present) is the way out of samsara. Paying attention to what is, prior to the mind that grasps or pushes away what is, is the way out.

One of the biggest obstacles to enlightenment, perhaps THE biggest, is ignoring direct experience.

This cannot be overstated, so don't underestimate it!

Enlightenment, or the simple realization-discovery of what you really are (that happens without the mind) can only "happen" in direct experience, not in your ideas about your direct experience.

The "direct" in direct experience points beyond the thinking mind to what is, that which is presently happening before the mind gets a hold of it, attempting to describe it, control it, label it or define it.

Direct experience is empty of all those movements of mind.

In direct experience, there is no interpreter of the moment.

Direct experience, believe it or not, happens outside of time, and it's always non-conceptual.

All these movements of mind are always past, while direct experience is always now.

And the eternal now, what you are, is the only "place" where Self-discovery is made.

Any clear insight that happens is actually in the immediacy of the moment. It is instantaneous and prior to any conceptualization whatsoever.

The natural state of being is wordless and everything is being registered and understood by the knowing presence that you are.

SEEING is happening all the time, non-conceptually, before the mind steps in to translate with words.

It is habitually ingrained in us to believe that the "me" and the mind's interpretation of reality is reality.

In pure SEEING, the "me" isn't present (as a thought) to get in the way. However, the "me" seems to be present when the mind steps in to translate what is happening with words and concepts.

But the 'me' never SEES. The "me" isn't the one seeing. There is ONE SEEING – and YOU ARE THAT.

So look at your direct experience, instead of your mind's interpretation of your direct experience.

Whatever you think direct experience is, it's not that. In fact, whatever you think it is *can't* be that. (Oh, the seeming contradictions that inevitably comes with language!)

"What is" can be said to be the "direct" in direct experience.

What is, or direct experience, is what is actually happening in any given moment, and never our assessment, evaluation or comparison of what is happening in any given moment.

In other words, it's before all that.

It's innocent, naked and pure, devoid of any conception whatsoever.

Even though it isn't a location or a place that can be found, it *is* where all healing and resolution ultimately happens.

And that's good news, because absolutely everything wants to heal and resolve itself (and come back home) in the light of real knowing.

Isn't this comforting to know? That absolutely every drama, trauma, struggle or wound that you presently struggle with *wants* to be resolved?

Waiting to be looked at, with the lights on.

The only reason these traumas, dramas and wounds are still in your experience is because you haven't given them enough single-pointed attention. Give them the proper loving attention, and they will fade.

If you want anything to leave your experience, it must be seen. I tell you, it *wants* to be seen.

Things can never be different than they are. They are often different than they were, and they will often be different than they will be, but they will never be different than they are – for all of eternity.

And so, all these unresolved places in you, all these feelings and sensations that weigh you down and make you afraid and uneasy, they simply want your attention. They crave your loving attention, the kind that doesn't shame or beat up.

I know this might be difficult for the "you" you think you are, but I'm not talking to that fictional one. I'm talking to YOU, the real YOU, the one that was never born and the one that will never die, that which the 'you' appears in.

Is there enough room in your heart to invite them all in? Because I can tell you that they are already being welcomed in as you read this. Yes, by YOU.

If you think you're the separate you, the one who was born and will one day die, this welcoming won't be sensed in your experience.

When the 'you' that you think you are runs from these places of contention, they will continue to haunt you. When the 'you' that you think you are argues with them, you will continue to suffer.

If you look at them directly in the eye while embracing them, you get to watch them eventually dissolve in (and by) your loving gaze.

For the quicker and direct route, realize what you really are, and witness them all dissolve in the light of loving awareness so fast you'll be amazed.

Seeing Through The 12 Biggest Obstacles To Enlightenment

This light *is* the ever-present now, not the now before the next now, and not the now after the last one, but this one, right now – this eternal, timeless now.

All your insecurities, self-esteem issues and emotional and psychological suffering all want to be resolved in the unshakeable knowing of who you really are, in this time-less now.

Upon the clear and unmistakable recognition of who you really are, beyond time and mind, all emotional and psychological suffering are immediately resolved.

Do you want that? I mean, do you *really* want that?

If so, stay in non-conceptual direct experience; don't ignore it.

This is where your freedom lies. Trust in it.

The author did, and now I AM writing You to remind You of what You've forgotten.

There is no resolution and healing in time. And remember, time is mind. If you are after the time-less, let the mind be.

Descriptions, words and opinions are conceptual, and there is no being in them.

You are behind the mind. You are that which the mind arises and sets in.

This light of real knowing is concept-free, immediately available, never leaves, is right where you ARE, and eternally outside the stream of time.

It's what you already ARE.

Do you realize that you look to the mind to tell you what is real and true?

Do you realize that whatever you are fascinated with you want? Do you realize that whatever you are fascinated with lives on in your experience?

When we are fascinated with our selves, we are fascinated with our fictions.

Have you considered that wisdom and real knowing resides below the neck, in your being?

If wisdom resides below the neck in being that already knows, why do you insist on referencing the mind to tell you what is true?

Take heart; you aren't doing any of it.

You think you are, but you aren't. Not even a little bit. Yes, it certainly appears that way, but this is a game of going beyond appearances and pulling back the curtain to see what (not who) is really pulling the levers.

It happens automatically and spontaneously, without you.

Present before thought, you ARE.

Prior to belief, assumption and opinion, you ARE.

Present before thought, direct experience resides.

Direct experience lives and moves independent of anything the mind can come up with, and anything life can throw at it.

What you say about what happens is a secondary overlay on top of direct experience, and because you believe it, it is this very overlay that is an obstacle to enlightenment.

See through the notion that notions can actually describe and define the actual, the indescribable.

If you need a reminder, go try to drink the word water.

A mere thought believed in has the power to pull the wool over your eyes for all eternity, preventing you from seeing that what you're looking for is what is looking!

Seeing Through The 12 Biggest Obstacles To Enlightenment

What you think, judge and resist are all overlays (heaped on top of direct experience) that cloud clear and direct seeing.

Direct seeing can only happen in direct experience, prior to thought.

Without referencing thought, what notices thought come and go?

Does that which notices thought come and go, or is it always Here?

Can you ever deny the fact that you exist? Can you ever deny the fact of your own being?

The knowledge of your real identity is here immediately in direct experience. The mind can't see this because it appears in that.

You ARE the immediacy of this moment.

You are present whether the mind appears or not.

Thinking, feeling, sensing and all other functioning happens spontaneously and effortlessly without the mind thinking about it. You are seeing right now, but are your eyes claiming, "I see?"

Seeing is already happening when "I see" is a thought.

When you say, "I am hearing" who is this "I" you are talking about? Hearing is already happening, effortlessly and spontaneously.

"I am hearing" is a thought.

When you say, "I am breathing," is this true?

When you say, "My heart is beating," is this true?

Thought happens in awareness directly, but the "I" is not present other than a concept.

What about the "you" that's being aware? Is the "you"

that's being aware as obvious as awareness being present?

Before thinking, judgment and resistance, these secondary overlays that are clouding the discovery of who you really are, you already ARE, without thought, judgment and resistance.

All that content arises in the naked, aware presence you are.

You're just looking in the wrong direction.

You are the thought-free space of empty, formless awareness that allows all thought forms to freely pass through.

You are the judgment-free space of empty, formless awareness that allows all judgment to freely pass through.

You are the resistance-free space of empty, formless awareness that allows all resistance to freely pass through.

You are the gender-less, age-less, welcoming space of awareness that allows all thought, emotion, sensation and experience to come and go in.

Indeed, You are the Host that equally invites all, without partiality, preference or condition.

As Host, you have no set time for "guests" to leave. Stay as long as you wish – and leave as early as you like.

It doesn't matter.

There is no purpose or agenda Here.

There are no demands or expectations Here.

No should or shouldn't Here.

No right or wrong, good or bad Here.

Life is the party.

All is Welcome – but only in direct experience.

Don't ignore where your freedom lies.

It is ever-present before thought.

If you look with the "I", you dream.

If you look for the "I", you awaken.

Chapter 7
It Can't Be *That* Simple!

To know the self as the only reality, and all else as temporal and transient is freedom, peace and joy. It is all very simple. Instead of seeing things as imagined, learn to see things as they are.

~ **Nisargadatta Maharaj**

One of the biggest obstacles to enlightenment is the belief that it must be a really complex thing to awaken to your true nature.

Once I was listening to a recording of a teacher and a student talking about the recognition of what they really are.

The student said, "The space of awareness that is present and aware of thoughts and feelings, that's it? That can't be it."

The teacher says, "Yes, that IS it. Do you think it's anything more than that?"

Dead silence.

The student obviously was stunned into silence and confused by the sheer simplicity of the answer she just received.

I just smiled, because I remember when I felt the same

way. I even remember saying to myself, *"That's* it?"

IT IS SO ORDINARY AND SIMPLE THAT IT LITERALLY BOGGLES THE MIND.

Do not think it is something special and extraordinary, with fireworks and balloons. Granted, the mind would love this, but it just isn't so.

THIS SILENT, EMPTY, AWARE SPACE OF AWARENESS that never comes and goes, that is eternally ever-present, IS what you really ARE.

While it is so simple, the realization of it is so beautifully wonderful.

What is the only thing that remains when all else goes?

What YOU are.

All else (phenomenon) comes and goes in what you are.

YOU are the Time-less, Formless Spirit that allows absolutely everything to be as it is, without preference or partiality.

"Let what comes come, let what goes go. Find out what remains."

If you continue to falsely identify with the mind (that which comes and goes within what you are) you will continue to suffer in life.

If you can notice the mind, wouldn't you have to be prior to the mind?

Don't answer because that would be just another concept; just See what is true in your direct experience prior to conceptualizing.

I can only imagine how many seekers were already resting in their true nature (feeling such a sense of peace and freedom) only for the mind to conclude that, "No, it can't be this simple.

This is so immediately available that it just can't be. It took no effort, so it has to be more than this!"

And pop, no more peace.

Believing it has to be more than that, on the path they continue.

We assume it takes a long journey filled with countless hours of looking within, peeling away layers of untruth, while pondering the nature of reality.

Reading stories about monks meditating in caves for years, people renouncing everything, including their jobs and families in order for 'it' to happen, hearing about seekers travelling to India from all parts of the globe all indicate a huge undertaking, right?

How can *that* be simple?

And geez, I wonder if I'm even worthy, wise and spiritual enough to begin with!

Believing in the seriousness of it all, off they go, out in search of what is already immediately available within, without ever turning a stone or lifting a finger.

Working through and systematically ascending all the levels (that must go with realizing one's true nature) has got to be pretty complex, right?

Since You are simply forgetting You, it is the mind that imagines what enlightenment must be like.

And for that reason, no wonder it thinks it must be complex.

The mind deals in complexity, not simplicity. The mind concludes that anything worthwhile has got be complex, or it wouldn't be worthwhile.

Anything worth achieving takes a lot of hard work, right?

However, clarity does not require retiring to forests and caves, or giving up all your material possessions. Simply abandon all your erroneous ideas and belief. All you suffer from is your belief system.

All the while truth remains simple – so simple in fact, the mind overlooks it.

And that's perfectly fine, because it isn't the mind that will recognize it.

This is about YOU recognizing YOU!

Truth is so simple that it is beyond all comprehension. It is immediate, before all seeking.

Awareness of seeking isn't seeking.

It can't be comprehended or apprehended by thought, as it is beyond thought, while simultaneously being the source and substance of thought.

It is ever present, displaying itself as every single facet of experience.

The mind can and usually does have some kind of intellectual understanding of what enlightenment is, but that understanding isn't it.

As much as it tries, thought (mind) can never approach this and therefore, it can never *be* what the mind thinks it is.

The mind certainly has the ability to imagine what enlightenment is, but the imagination of it isn't it, either.

It's not what the mind hears it is, nor is it what the mind has read about what it is.

Being eternally kept out of the loop, the mind doesn't know that liberation isn't *about* the mind – and that it isn't *for* the mind.

And it certainly doesn't know that it can't be realized *by*

Seeing Through The 12 Biggest Obstacles To Enlightenment

the mind.

Upon awakening, it is validated that it was never about the mind!

So in the meantime, let the mind do what it will.

Contrary to what you may have heard, the contents of the mind are not relevant.

The mind will dismiss the transformative, 15-word pointer it just read, but I am telling YOU, don't.

Since the mind cannot fathom or imagine what it is, it has a tendency to lose interest rather quickly.

Because it is so radically simple, it loses interest.

And this isn't a bad thing, because I'm not asking you to look with the mind.

What else is there you may ask? YOU, the aware presence that gives rise to the mind.

When it is heard that the discovery of your Real Identity (which is no identity at all) won't happen with thought, something of a higher order can move in.

You just made room.

You can't replace your old worn out couch until you make room for the new one, can you? (Unless you want a cluttered living room!)

See through the thought obstacle that says the realization of what you really are is complex.

It isn't.

Not even a little bit.

It is so radically simple that it's literally mind-blowing.

Enlightenment is nothing other than the clear recognition and remembrance of what you really are, not who you think or believe you are.

Once it is clearly seen, all doubt about what you are is forever removed.

Liberation is seeing that there was no one present to be in bondage in the first place.

It is much simpler than you realize!

This is not something you 'get' because there is no "you" present at the scene to get anything.

Without referring to thought or sensation, what do you discover when you do a simple investigation?

What is always here?

What is discovered is a Being-Awareness that is the ultimate backstop of all experience.

It is the simple and undeniable fact of being, which is always and already beyond doubt.

And because it is so subtle and unremarkable, it's easily overlooked.

Sometimes the best place to hide something is in the most obvious of places.

YOU "hid" this closer than breathing, nearer than hands and feet, yet with the intention of discovering it.

Look right now in direct experience.

Notice that before the mind translates what is happening, there is a motion of wordless SEEING that registers everything that is happening.

You are this AWARE SEEING, the knowing principle that never leaves.

Chapter 8
Even More Than Fear

To live in the Great Way is neither easy nor difficult, but those with limited views are fearful and irresolute: the faster they hurry, the slower they go, and clinging cannot be limited: even to be attached to the idea of enlightenment is to go astray. Just let things be in their own way and there will be neither coming nor going. Obey the nature of things (your own nature), and you will walk freely and undisturbed.

~ Hsin Hsin Ming

Most would say that if you got to the core issue, the thing that holds people back from awakening is fear.

On the surface of things, this seems to be true.

Generally, fear catches the blame for the thing that holds us back from achieving anything in life. It keeps us standing still, paralyzed from moving in the direction we intuitively know is real and true.

It's a pretty normal experience to fear what we most want.

I considered writing a chapter on fear and how it can

Seeing Through The 12 Biggest Obstacles To Enlightenment

serve as an obstacle to awakening to your natural state, but decided against it due to all the books already written about fear.

Suffice it to say that fear naturally arises because the mind doesn't want to be seen for the phantom it is. It would lose its job as Master if consciousness wakes up to itself.

Let fear arise, it can't hurt you. Let fear arise; it's only energy.

But even more than fear, the will to control is even a bigger obstacle, often keeping us on a treadmill of confusion and angst.

Fear arises when you think you have no control. Therefore, control is the main obstacle that gets in the way.

The desire and will to control presupposes that Life needs help, that Being doesn't already know the way.

The fear-based mind thinks *it* knows the way.

The need to control presupposes we aren't enough as we are, and that we need to manipulate what is in order to arrive at the awakened state of being.

But if what you already are (without condition, time or improvement) is perfect, whole and complete already, does it make any sense at all that *any* form of control is needed?

How do you arrive at the effortless, eternal space of awareness with journeys in time, filled with effort and control?

Does it make sense to use effort to land in the effortless?

Does it make sense to control in order to get to the uncontrolled space you are?

If you were able to give up all control on every level, you would be a free being.

Free of the desire to control, you find yourself with a very different experience of yourself, others and the world.

The willingness to rest completely and totally in the unknown, this moment right now, is tantamount to giving up all control.

When you give up control to have things your way in the only point of power (right now – it is always right now) you allow for another possibility to arise, the kind that transforms a life and ushers in a wondrous realization.

Do not resist or control any part of your experience, for your experience happens inside. When you resist what is, as is, that negative energy has nowhere to go. It stays within you.

Allowing what is, as is, nothing remains but the uncontaminated You.

We want permanence, yet all things are impermanent. Not seeing this simple truth is the cause of so much pain and suffering.

By showing up innocently (without demand) in this unknowable moment, it is seen that there is nothing to cling to, and nothing to grab hold of.

Seeing that there is nothing to grasp, no longer do you cling to the known to tell you what is true.

Seeing that no thought is ultimately true, no longer do you reference the thinking mind to tell you what is real and true.

Like a clenched fist can never hold water, with a relaxed and open hand, water comes to rest in your palm.

In this relaxed and open state, You start to get glimpses of the eternal, and it's none other than YOU.

The desire to control is essentially a postponement strategy that keeps you from awakening to your true nature as Aware, Awake Spirit.

Aren't fear and resistance forms of control, too?

While it's true that you don't decide to be in fear, and

while it's true that you don't consciously decide to resist, know that they are both mind-generated attempts to survive and remain in the driver's seat.

When these contractions we call fear and resistance arise, simply notice it. Often, the clear seeing of something is the letting go of it.

But you don't have to let go of anything because there is no-thing to hold on to. Everything is in a constant state of flux and decay and therefore, this letting go is already done for you.

But the most relevant and transformative thing to inquire is this: what notices these attempts by the mind?

What is that?

Wouldn't *that* have to be prior, in order to notice these contractions?

Does that which notices have any need to control and protect?

Isn't the awareness of fear and control *eternally free* of fear and control?

If what you already are is perfect peace and surrender, a lover of what is, and not a lover of what could or should be, does it make any sense that control and effort are needed to rest in what you already are?

If you identify who you are as the thinking mind, doesn't it make perfect sense that you'd feel control and manipulation is needed in your experience?

Mind, being all about control, isn't really keen on what is.

What is tends to be ordinary and often boring to the mind. The mind thinks it can improve and make what is presently happening better and more pleasing.

What is just doesn't seem attractive to the mind.

YOU are a lover of what is; mind (who you think you are)

isn't.

How about agreeing and disagreeing?

Aren't they also forms of control?

It is the mind that agrees and disagrees, sometimes vehemently and passionately, with the obvious aim of control.

Don't delay the seeing of what you really are by referencing the memory of past and/or comparing what you think you know against what is being pointed out to you now.

This postponement strategy is a form of control and a terrific obstacle to enlightenment.

Waiting for seeing or enlightenment is a delay tactic because it puts off dis-identifying with the thinking mind; it puts off seeing that you are the space the mind arises in.

And belief in thought is the glue that holds identification together.

When these movements of mind happen, simply see them and let them be.

The important thing to see is that all these empty thoughts arise and appear in the thought-less, clear, space of awareness that you really are.

Once you begin to get glimpses of your actual nature as pure awareness, in which the mind and all else appears and disappears, the will to control tends to die down significantly.

All that effort and struggle that coincided with mind identification dies down in the clear recognition that You are already free – and the remembrance that you never needed to *become* free starts to radiantly shine through.

The thoughts that bind and immobilize us all have their root in the initial thought of separation, the "I" thought. Until this is clearly seen through, the mind will continue to try to control and give trouble.

See this, and in one fell swoop, wipe away an entire lifetime investment in beliefs and concepts rooted in self-centered activity, the self that never existed in the first place.

See this one thing and the enslavement of the mind is resolved.

Before the mind, you ARE.

Present before thought, you ARE.

Realize that the mind never was the enemy and never had any real and ultimate power. It was just doing its thing, doing what mind is designed to do, all in the untouched, impersonal space of awareness that you ARE.

All along you thought you were the mind, and naturally, as the mind went, you went.

The cure for what ails you (temporary ignorance) is wisdom, or clear seeing. This clear seeing undercuts the mind, without any personal effort at all.

Once this is pointed out by a qualified teacher (which is how it usually goes down) your own seeing kicks in and you are able to take it from there.

The goal of the true teacher is to help you get to the point where this seeing takes hold so that you no longer have to rely on him or her for anything, even confirmation that clear seeing indeed has taken place.

The wisdom (or recognition arising in you) is the inevitable response to recognizing and remembering the truth being point out.

Your own innate wisdom is awakening and wants you to see what needs to be seen.

The innate higher intelligence within you is so much greater than the thinking mind. You know this but have forgotten, so have faith and stay with the pointers, letting them hit home.

Remember, You allowed your Self to forget your Self, but only in order to remember your Self.

When fear arises (and oh, it will) let it be there without trying to make it go away. When resistance arises (oh, it most certainly will) let it be there without trying to un-resist.

The 'letting it be' in your experience (without trying to change it or will it away) is the dissolving agent. This is not a doing, nor does it take effort.

Since there is absolutely nothing you can do about it, relax and let it unfold naturally, because you can't make it happen.

No control needed. You're not driving the bus anyway. You just think you are.

Simply allow what is.

Allow what is, all the way up to awakening.

Once your own seeing starts to open up and take hold, knowing moves to the irreversible point of being unshakeable.

Where doubt never arises anymore.

Where problems don't exist.

Where improvements aren't needed.

Where you aren't free of emotion, but free *from* emotion.

You know that you know, and the need for teachers and books like this fade away.

The most important thing is to keep looking at what is being pointed to (without giving a verbal answer – which is a mere concept created by mind) until you see it for yourself and know it for certain.

That which is always here, this alive, presence of awareness (that never comes and goes) forever remains when all else doesn't.

This realization will become stable and doubt will never arise anymore – ever.

This impartial awareness that witnesses all passing thought, emotion and sensation is the substratum that remains untouched and unharmed by temporary appearances.

It's like when you throw black paint in the air, the air remains uncontaminated. You never color the air black. Regardless of what happens to you, YOU remain untouched and at peace.

This is what you really ARE, your Real Nature.

The Consciousness that is peering through your eyes right now is already free.

There is no other understanding or realization beyond this. You exist and you already know you exist – and all the teacher does is assure you of this by continually pointing you back to this.

Everything happens as it happens; it is only the mind that judges, labels and evaluates things as 'good' and "bad," "pleasant" and "unpleasant."

Everything arises and sets in the light of your being, without anything being separate from that.

Forms continuously appear and disappear, with nothing ever being gained or lost.

All appears from that, exists in that, and dissolves back into that.

You are both the Source and Substance of all that is seen and unseen.

You are the Unseen Seer of all that is seen, the Unknown Knower of all that is known.

You are the Form-less that informs and witness all passing form.

You are the Unborn that gives birth to all that is born.

You are the Radiant, ever-present background that everything comes and goes in.

And despite the appearance to the contrary, you have no control over anything.

Realize that life is perfect here and now, and that you never once left the peace and freedom that you've been seeking.

Though you won't ever find You, see your Self as the uncreated, unconditioned, conscious awareness that is unharmed and untouched by all.

It really is this simple.

Nail down your identity and all else is resolved in the unshakeable knowing of who you really are.

Dismiss needless, mind-generated will and control, manipulation and management, and rest in what you already are.

No effort needed.

You wouldn't trade a billion dollars for seeing this.

Chapter 9
Caught In Dualism

Enlightenment is the realization of completeness. It's the seeing of God equally in all, seeing the perfection of all, the completeness of all and therefore, the non-separation of all. Dare you see it?

~ **Adyashanti**

Nature is the best teacher. Henry David Thoreau said nature never apologizes, and it's because nature doesn't have any concept of right and wrong, ugly and beautiful, and this and that.

It's evident that some of the things we call "opposites" do appear to exist in nature. For example, there are big fish and small fish, large rocks and small rocks, mature trees and immature trees – with sickly leaves and healthy leaves.

But it isn't problematic for them. It doesn't toss them into fits of rage or attacks of panic. Perhaps there are dumb hippos and smart hippos, but it doesn't seem to bother them much. You just don't find inferiority complexes in hippos.

Similarly, there is both life and death in nature, but it doesn't seem to terrify nature like it does humans. An old cat isn't caught up in fear and anxiety over its impending death.

Seeing Through The 12 Biggest Obstacles To Enlightenment

When its time has come, it gracefully moves to a secluded corner, curls up and goes to sleep one last time.

An ill sparrow that knows its time is near, perches quietly on a branch and stares off into the distance at its last sunset.

When it sees the light no more, it closes its eyes one final time, and without any drama or fanfare, falls gently to the ground below. It's all so natural.

But with humans, this isn't the case. Getting humans to see that the death of the body is natural is very difficult. We do anything to avoid the topic, and we'll do anything to prolong this inevitable event.

When your mind and body inevitably die, YOU still remain.

Before the body was born, YOU ARE.

You were never born and you will never die. You are the One life appearing as (insert your name here). You don't exist as a separate entity anyway. Look within and tell me where you are.

The false cannot stand up to examination – it just can't.

Let me ask you: Can anything happen without consciousness? If nothing happens without consciousness, then everything must happen within consciousness, right?

Not only is this logical, but it can be confirmed in direct experience, where the proof is in the pudding.

If everything happens within consciousness, nothing is external to you.

You can only look within because absolutely nothing is outside You. Look up into the sky, universes are within You.

No matter how hard you try, you can never get outside, because there isn't an outside.

No matter how hard you try, there is no escaping

Oneness.

While it appears that things are separate and outside of you, everything happens within what you are – even the death of the body.

So the next time you look up at the moon on a clear, star-filled night, look and see if the moon is actually separate and external to you.

The realization-discovery of what you really are is all about going beyond appearances, that is, if you don't want to be stuck *in* appearances.

The mind and its content are appearances in what you are. The same goes for emotions, sensations and experience.

We can accurately say that absolutely everything is an appearance in what you are. Appearances arise within you and are temporal. You are not an appearance. You are the eternal spaciousness all appears in.

How can an appearance touch what you are, the space of awareness that precedes all appearance? Only if there is a belief in the appearance (as real) can it seemingly harm what you are.

What you ARE can never be harmed or threatened.

There is no reference point present that you can call "you" that can be harmed.

It's not your fault that you believe you can be harmed; you were taught from birth to believe in this false idea.

Take solace in the fact that more than ninety-nine percent still do. If seeing this were easy, there'd be millions already awake.

Because the mind can only think in terms of duality, it makes sense that while we identify who we are with the mind, we'll be caught in dualism.

Wake up from the mind that believes in duality and enjoy

the seeming opposites that arise together.

This is where the fun is.

The truth is, there is no separate entity living in a separate world.

It just appears that way.

Enlightenment can only happen once it is seen that duality is the illusion, not the reality. Nothing really "happens" other than the recognition of what is already the case.

The One created the mind to divide and separate, to only think in terms of duality. If it were not for this, experience couldn't happen.

Without the potential for opposing experiences, any experience isn't possible.

Could you really experience joy and happiness if it weren't for the experience of pain and suffering?

Could you experience inner peace if it weren't for inner turmoil?

What might happen if we see the conditions of existence as mutually interdependent on each other, as the quantum physicists have already proven?

When you're happy, can you begin to see how being grateful for pain and suffering makes sense?

In the phenomenal world of form, of things seen, things are either now or then, this or that, here or there, up or down, hot or cold, good or bad, right or wrong, and pleasant or unpleasant.

The opposites arise together, and while they do so simultaneously, the actual reality is Non-dual, without an opposite.

The Non-dual is the ground of being that cradles the dual, or the appearance of the dual.

You are the non-dual presence of awareness that all seeming duality arises and sets in.

Without the appearance of dualism, Oneness couldn't exist.

The One appears as two, in order to experience itself.

If we look behind the appearance to the underlying essence, we see non-duality, or not two, the singular animating essence of all.

YOU ARE THAT SINGULAR ESSENCE – not a "part" of it, but ALL of it, wholly and completely.

The One, Singular Essence that is looking through your eyes right now is the same ONE that is looking through the eyes of every other body.

The love that sustains the mind/body YOU are driving around in is the same love that sustains not only every other body, but every blade of grass, flower blooming, dog barking, cat meowing, star shining and hurricane destroying.

Without YOU, nothing is. Without YOU, the Singular ground of being, opposites don't arise and therefore, nothing else does either.

The function of the mind is to divide where there is no division anywhere to be found.

In truth, opposites aren't either "good" or "bad", "right" or wrong"; they just are.

So while non-duality is the reality, until we wake up to the truth *of* reality, we'll be forever ensnared *by* duality.

We could say that the belief in duality (as the reality) is the force that spins the wheel of suffering. To get off the wheel of suffering and samsara is to see that they in fact arise simultaneously as one.

Most of our problems come from believing that the

opposites can and should be separated from one another. Most of our shame and insecurity comes from our resisting (and running from) our 'flawed' and negative aspects, while embracing our 'attractive' and positive aspects.

Realizing that all opposites are actually aspects of one, underlying reality, we see through the illusion of duality and free ourselves from the pairs of opposites.

In this seeing, we are liberated from the nonsensical challenges that are involved in the war of opposites.

Recognizing that the point was never to pit one side against the other in search of peace, we unify and harmonize the polarities by discovering the ground that encompasses both.

Resting in this ground that equally includes both, we inevitably transcend both.

Until we see that we are the ONE, formless, unconditioned consciousness behind and prior to the mind, we will forever be identified with the contents of the conditioned mind that accumulates ad infinitum.

As the mind goes, we go.

When we think peace isn't present right now, we identify with turmoil – and we suffer.

When we think we need to manufacture peace, we assume it isn't already present.

The reality is peace is always present in our experience; it's just that our focus is on the non-peace.

When our focus is on the non-peace, peace eludes us even though it is fully present.

Liberation lies in the transcending of polarities, while simultaneously including the polarities.

Transcend and include is the way, not transcend and reject. It isn't possible to transcend *while* you reject. It just doesn't work that way.

We can only transcend *when* we include all of it.

Work with yourself, not against yourself.

In any moment, we can either reject or allow.

If what we reject can only bind us further, why not simply allow?

Allow what is and you are free.

Notice that which in you that already allows what is.

You ARE allowing, not someone who allows.

You ARE surrender, not someone who surrenders.

This is the real game changer, the noticing of what already is.

Don't "be here now" either.

This pointer has driven so many earnest seekers mad.

This pointer implies dividing lines and boundaries where there are none.

Is there a "you'" that can be here now?

Where do 'you' begin and end, and where does "now" begin and end?

Without referring to thought, can this alleged dividing line be found?

It's a dualistic perspective; don't get caught.

No longer believing in the existence of boundaries, separation and division fall away.

There isn't a now – nor is there a present moment.

There is just what is happening, eternally.

Be free and simply rest in This.

Don't say, "I need to become more present."

Is there a "you" that can become more present?

Isn't this just more duality?

These are just delay tactics created and sustained by the mind that wants to survive.

It doesn't want YOU to remember who YOU are.

It's really afraid of this, because then it's out of a job, the job of the master, the one in control.

It doesn't want to be the servant.

It fears being the servant because then it would lose control.

And the mind is all about control.

And as long as it is the master, you'll never be truly happy.

I know you want to be happy. It's a natural impulse.

Simply discover what you really are, and it will be realized that happiness is your natural state – and you'll never suffer again.

Happiness is the natural state of little children, to whom the kingdom belongs, that is, until they've been polluted by the insanity of society.

To acquire happiness you don't have to do anything, because happiness can't be acquired. How can you acquire what is deep at your core?

If you don't experience happiness, it's because you believe in things that aren't true.

You need nothing to be happy. You need something to be sad.

Jesuit priest Anthony deMello said, *"Life is easy, life is wonderful. It's only hard on your illusions, your ambitions, your greed and your cravings. Do you know where these things come from? From having identified with the separate self."*

Over the last seventy-five plus years, the self-help movement that spits out countless books, lectures, seminars and courses continues to the feed the notion that there is a self that needs help, that needs improving.

And yet, there is ONLY ONE, and YOU ARE THAT.

Don't overlook the truly amazing and wonderful implications of Non-duality AS THE REALITY.

It is staggering, and it will blow your mind.

Reality is all there is.

What appears is the appearance of that.

Given that there is no duality in the first place, nor any separate individual standing apart from that, who or what is present to embody anything?

The whole idea of embodiment implies a separation in reality. It's another dualistic perspective.

It is all life. Life is expressing itself as the entire universe.

In many cases, mere lip service is being paid to the non-existence of the "I", but it comes back in the form of "my awakening", "my embodiment", and "I'm not there yet."

What are the implications that there isn't a "you" *and* a world? That there isn't a separate "you" to be found anywhere?

That there is no "other" – and that there really isn't a dividing line anywhere other than in our minds?

See through this seeming obstacle, ponder the reality that it is all ONE, and realize you're already free with nothing to embody.

In this space, where time is no longer sensed, we sense

oneness with everything, without any boundary between our selves and what we see.

The less conscious we are, the more divided we are.

The more divided we are, the more we believe in dividing lines.

And the more we believe in dividing lines, the more we suffer.

The two are one, and there's not a snowball's chance in hell anyone could convince us otherwise.

Chapter 10
Hey, Where Did I Go?

If you let your attention go to your ear, you'll feel that it is constantly grasping. It is the same with the eye, the mind and all your organs. Let the grasping go and you will find your whole body is spontaneously an organ of sensitivity. The ear is merely a channel for this global sensation. It is not an end of itself. What is heard is also felt, seen, smelled and touched. Your five senses, intelligence and imagination are freed and come into play. You feel it is being completely expanded in space, without center or border. The ego, which is a contraction, can find no hold in this presence, and anxiety, like and dislike dissolve.

~ *Jean Klein*

When you start to get real close to realizing your true nature, you start to lose track of yourself for a while.

You take short vacations, and nowhere can you be found.

You've gone missing, and you start to think you should be on the back of milk cartons nationwide with the words, "Have You Seen Me?" plastered across the back.

Where once everything was being referenced back to you,

whether you liked or disliked what was happening, whether you preferred something else to be happening, this lifelong, believed in reference point begins to fade.

And then fade some more.

At first, it's kind of strange; it almost feels like an out-of-body experience.

It's peaceful.

It's spacious.

And it's relaxing.

You discover that you're most present when you're most absent.

You discover that you're most absent when you're most present.

This is the mystery of being conscious; we are ultimately un-findable, but obviously aware.

Isn't it interesting how much peace is felt in these scenarios, when "you" aren't there?

Then there is a tendency for fear to creep in. When you feel afraid, that's typically a good indicator you're close.

In truth, you already are what you are (and you can't get "close" to what you are) but in terms of sensory experience, "close" isn't such a bad way to put it.

Words aren't the actual; they just point. What in you is aware of words and concepts?

That's what the words are pointing to – that space of awareness that notices words and concepts.

In the end, the answer is not found in the mind because you already are the answer. It is the non-conceptual recognition that awareness is always present, and what is always present is aware.

Seeing Through The 12 Biggest Obstacles To Enlightenment

The 'answer' is in the clear seeing that when you look for the separate self and you find it entirely absent, YOU LET THAT REALIZATION SINK IN, despite what the mind says.

And trust me, the mind will have something to say about this; it does not want to be exposed as the Great Pretender, the one who thinks he's the captain steering the ship.

The last two things it wants: for you to stop believing you ARE the mind, and for you to stop referencing it for truth or reality.

So you're feeling this wonderful expanse of freedom where you seem to vanish for a bit – and then pop, fear arises and you're back in your body.

You're back in you.

The peace is gone. That spacious feeling of relaxation is gone.

You wonder why fear suddenly became your experience when you were just feeling so at peace.

You may be unaware that the mind can only take so much peace and relaxation before it needs to take back control.

You aren't aware that ego is trying to reassert itself, because it has a great fear of relinquishing control. If it doesn't feel present at the scene, you can bet it fears losing control.

Granted, it makes sense that fear will arise when "you" disappear. However, if the pointer is "you never existed in the first place," don't run and hide when fear presents itself.

Remain where you are and look and see if there is a "you" who experiences fear.

What is more real in direct evidence? A "you" who experiences fear, or simply fear being experienced?

All the while, who you REALLY are sits back in delight, watching it all unfold.

But if you still think you are the body/mind, there is no delight happening.

For no apparent reason, you just went from peace to panic in a matter of moments.

It's okay. It's understandable.

And it's very normal.

So don't sweat it.

Or wish it were any different than it is.

Allow what is.

The "you" who you think you are fears being annihilated.

It doesn't want to disappear like Houdini.

The key thing to see is that there never was a "you" present to be lost in the first place.

The "you"... that separate entity you think you are, is merely a thought believed in.

In other words, there isn't a "you" to be lost, because there was never a "you" to begin with.

What disappears is the firm conviction that you are a separate entity living in this world – that you are a body-mind with name and form.

What follows is the resurrection of the recognition of what you've always been.

Nothing's been lost except your false identity – and the mind doesn't like this.

If you have an entire lifetime invested in the "you" you think you are, with all its hopes, dreams, goals and plans for "your" life, don't you think it makes perfect sense for this "you" to be in fear of no longer existing?

Of course it's freaked out!

When this lifelong reference point called "me" that has been constantly improved upon and worked on eventually crumbles into the clear seeing of what you really are, laughter and relief generally arises.

But I say laugh now!

When it is eventually seen (by no one) that egos never get enlightened (because they never really existed in the first place other than a thought) you finally understand why Buddha tilted his head to the sky and let out a huge belly laugh!

You 'get' the joke when identification with the separate self falls away.

It is one big cosmic joke... and it's on YOU.

So don't let the fear of losing the "you" that never existed in the first place deter the recognition of who you really are.

Let fear come, let fear go.

It's only energy anyway – energy arising from false beliefs and false identifications.

And when this fear arises, let IT be a reminder to ask, "Where is this perception coming from?"

The fact is, YOU never disappear.

In fact, YOU are the only "thing" that never disappears. All else appears and disappears in YOU.

Aside from a thought, there was never anyone present to disappear in the first place.

Chapter 11
Guru Speak And Jive Talk

Re-examine all you have been told in school, in church or in any book, and dismiss whatever insults your soul, and your very flesh shall become a great poem, and have the richest fluency, not only in its words, but in the silent lines of its lips and face, and between the lashes of your eyes, and in every motion and joint of your body.

~ Walt Whitman

This chapter may ruffle some feathers, but I've never been too concerned with being politically correct, so let's continue, shall we?

Since the beginning, teachers have been doing a great disservice to the earnest seeker by perpetuating popular myths of enlightenment and disseminating false information.

Whether this is being done intentionally or not doesn't make it any less significant. In some cases, these so-called gurus do great damage to the student, both psychologically and emotionally.

Unfortunately, some never recover.

I say this not to alarm, but to point out that just because

someone takes on the role of "teacher" doesn't necessarily mean that what is being taught can be absolutely and unequivocally relied upon.

In other words, it doesn't necessarily mean that what is being conveyed is steeped in a deep realization of truth.

In many cases the student has a strong tendency to unconsciously gives credence to the teacher simply because they are in the role of teacher.

It's not uncommon for many teachers to sit in a nice big, fluffy chair elevated in the front of the room, in flowing spiritual garb surrounded by flowers. They speak to the students that sit lower in ordinary chairs.

I am not saying there is anything wrong with this. I have been in this situation many times as a seeker, and to this day, I am eternally grateful to the authentic teachers who pointed the way for me – whether they were elevated or not.

What I am suggesting is that if you find yourself in this scenario, be aware of what's going on within. Be aware of what the mind is concluding.

The important thing to know is that what they are, YOU are, without condition.

No hierarchy, no division, no special, no worthy and unworthy – and definitely no such thing as spiritual and un-spiritual. These are manmade concepts created in the mind, without any validity whatsoever.

Yet if we infer this division, and we believe in this apparent hierarchy, the mind is inclined to think that the teacher is "special" and more "spiritual" than we are.

And this just isn't so.

It doesn't automatically mean that the teacher is purposely trying to achieve this. They may or may not be, but again, I am not suggesting that when this scenario plays out, it's always a deliberate ploy to get you to place the teacher on a pedestal.

The important thing is to be aware *not* to create the obstacle that says, "The teacher is special, I am not." It is important to be aware *not* to create the obstacle that says, "I don't have what the teacher has and therefore, I want what the teacher has."

There is only ONE, without any separation, and you are THIS ONE, without condition.

See this and be free.

You already are (wholly and completely) what you seek for.

Believe it until you realize it; this is a good example for when a belief is useful.

Once this is clearly seen and recognized, no longer will you elevate anything aside from your ankle after you sprained it, or your arm while you give a toast!

What I AM, YOU ARE.

And then you have a certain segment of teachers who are nothing more than enlightened egos, devoid of any real and true self-realization, manipulating seekers for their own personal profit and gain.

This gain could come in the form of money, sex, fame and adulation, approval and a whole host of other things. In the end, they are all self-centered motivations.

Naturally, there are things conveyed that are much less damaging, like meditation being necessary to awaken to your true nature, or breathing exercises (pranayama) and singing mantras to help facilitate awakening.

In no way am I against these practices as I did my fair share of them. I'm just saying they aren't essential to the realization of what you are. Can it "happen" while engaging in these practices? Sure, anything is possible, but it isn't necessary.

Does present awareness need meditation in order to be? Does silence and quiet need to be created in order to see the simple fact that awareness is the substratum of all sound and noise?

All techniques stem from the level of the mind, while what you are delights in your attempts to employ techniques in order to see what you already are.

What you are is the very awareness that the idea "I need to meditate or do breathing exercises in order to realize my true nature" arises in.

Meditation can be very useful, especially physiologically, mentally and emotionally. It has a calming effect on the system like nothing else. Therefore, if you are drawn to it (breathing exercises and mantras, too), then by all means, sit in silence and let whatever arises arise. Do your pranayama, and sing your bhajans.

But they aren't ultimately needed to realize what you Really are.

We breathe in a specific way and sing certain mantras as long as we're not totally clear on what we are. Nothing wrong with this; it's just what is happening.

Who needs to manufacture quiet when it is noticed that quiet is always and already present?

Aren't the byproducts of meditation (peace and silence) already here, naturally and spontaneously?

Look right now in your own direct experience and see if this is true or not. And if you're having difficulty seeing this, pay attention to the silence between thoughts, and the silence between the noises you may hear.

So before "you" go and meditate to bring about peace and

calm you think isn't present, look and see if it's not already present.

And isn't this more duality anyway – a separate entity needing to create silence?

See what is already the case.

Silence isn't something that needs to be created or practiced; it's what you are.

"Silence is not the absence of sound, but the absence of self."

The silent, aware, awake presence you are is sensed just as easily right now as it is in meditation.

Know this and be at peace.

We search and meditate as long as we are not crystal clear that what we are seeking for we already are. There is nothing wrong with this. It's just happening.

Relax in this that you are, the ever-present witnessing awareness of all that comes and goes.

You already are the clear, knowing, silent, aware presence in which all appearances, thoughts and emotions rise and set in.

Can you deny the fact of being, ever? Is there ever a time that you are not?

Can you imagine not existing? (Don't skip this one.)

Some gurus say that thought ceases upon awakening. Granted, the mind quiets down quite a bit, but thinking never stops until the body dies.

Don't get caught by this one.

After all, you aren't the one doing the thinking. You are not the author of thinking. Thinking happens all by itself. Thinking never touches what you are.

Another fallacy is that the mind must be purified first.

Seeing Through The 12 Biggest Obstacles To Enlightenment

This is pure folly and anyone who suggests so is simply mistaken or intentionally misleading you. Nothing needs to be purified.

Awakening isn't about the mind – at all.

This is about YOU, that which is behind and prior to the mind. This is about YOU, that which is the source and substance *of* the mind.

The mind doesn't wake up. This is about waking up *from* the mind. Once this happens, you won't give a hoot what the mind says again – ever.

Even though the mind often gets a bad rap, it can come along for the ride. It isn't the bogeyman.

But where is this mind you believe in? Can you find it? Can you pinpoint its actual location, where "it" starts and ends? Can you find its boundary line, you know, where it ends and all else begins?

If you have an answer, it's just the mind, The Big Divider, spitting out yet another conceptual dividing line and reference point where there aren't *any* to be found.

There is no (actual) mind apart from thinking. Can you grasp anything that you can call "mind?"

Mind is just a movement of energy, patterns coming and going spontaneously, in the aware presence you are, as long as breathing is occurring.

When the body dies, so does thinking.

If it dies, was it real to begin with? If it's not real, can truth be found in it?

So why do you identify with that which dies? Why do you reference the dying mind to tell you what is real and true?

When thought stops, where is the mind?

When thought stops, do you cease to exist?

The mind, like death, is a concept believed in.

The good news is that the mind (what mind?) does quiet down significantly after awakening. At least this is the author's experience.

Confusing mystical experiences with enlightenment is a common myth that has seekers dizzy, running around in circles.

Mystical experiences, like kundalini awakenings, where your body shakes uncontrollably, or seeing visions of the blue pearl or white, golden lights also have nothing to do with truth and awakening.

They're just experiences with a beginning, middle, and end. You are not an experience. You are the empty, aware container in which experience happens in.

My chakras were intensely awakened by a teacher from India in 2001. Sitting upright in a chair for about twenty minutes, a violin played in the background and my upper body danced and swayed, moving in sync with each note.

It was though I was being played, literally.

It continued on and off for about eighteen months and admittedly, things began to quicken and more clarity was the experience. But again, this is not requisite.

Many awaken without ever experiencing these kinds of things.

They are nice experiences and sometimes very pleasurable, but they are not essential to awakening. They definitely don't make you any more spiritual or holier than the next guy or gal.

So don't think they are necessary. They are not. Do not be disappointed if they don't happen to you – and don't be concerned if they don't happen to you. If they happen, enjoy them. Like all other experiences, they won't last.

Besides, You are after the timeless.

The discovery of your true nature, waking up to your real identity is NOT an experience among many other experiences, and it definitely doesn't depend on you having any particular experience.

So don't go looking for ANY particular experience.

What you are is the EVER-PRESENT state-less state, prior to and behind all experience, where all states and experience come and go in.

Thinking only bliss remains when you wake up is another one.

Everlasting bliss (upon awakening) is perhaps the most common myth perpetuated and one I find the most humorous. Anyone who pretends to give the impression that they are in a constant state of peace and joy isn't being genuine.

There is no constant state of peace and joy that any man or woman walks around in upon awakening.

Talk about misleading – this is mere jive talk – even better than the Bee Gees could do!

Bliss seems to imply some heightened state of euphoria or ecstasy. Like all other emotional states, it is impermanent and on the move. If you think bliss will forever remain, you're in for a big surprise.

The nice part is, You won't care anyway.

As long as we're in human form with thoughts and emotions, it's just not possible to be in bliss all the time. It might be nice, but it's just not realistic.

As mentioned before, the mind does quiet down a tremendous amount, and insecurity and confusion drops away, but 'negative' emotions can (and do) still arise.

Awareness, on the other hand, is more of a sustained and

steady peace – an unwavering, bulletproof sense of wellness that never leaves and is never harmed.

So while the body and mind may be experiencing negative emotions, there is an ever-present sense of wellbeing in the background. This is what you are, the eternal background of peace that non-peace appears in.

Rest in this Background of Being that you ARE. You are the Effortless Okayness that all "happens" in.

After awakening or enlightenment, things will go on as they did before, but for no one. Painful experiences still happen, sad and angry emotions still arise from time to time, but there is no resistance to them anymore.

Experiences come and they are allowed to happen, like clouds floating by in a vast, empty sky. As a result, they don't stick around long. Like clouds, they appear for a bit and are felt, and then dissipate.

There is a transparency felt now, where sensations come in the front and go out the back, without sticking in the middle. Sometimes there is a sticking in the middle, but not for very long.

Without the filter of the mind, life is experienced deeper and richer. Without the filter of the mind, often you feel things more. It's perfectly okay because there is no longer any resistance *to* what is happening.

You just allow what is. Rather, all is being allowed, by itself, without any conscious decision to do so.

The resistance TO pain was the very mechanism that brought about suffering, right behind the belief in a separate entity that *could* suffer.

All is allowed in the open, unfettered space of awareness you are.

There is no resistance to inevitable pain anymore and consequently, suffering doesn't arise. It's been over ten years since the last time suffering was experienced here.

My chocolate lab died three months ago and grief was felt for about four weeks, and then sadness for about seven-eight more. Sometimes I think of her and tears still well up, like right now.

Never in a million years did I think that a dog's passing would break my heart wide open. My love for her will never fade – and unless I get Alzheimer's one day – her beautiful face and sound of her bark will always be clear in my mind's eye.

But never once did I suffer because all that grief and sadness was never resisted.

It was allowed, every bit of it. And "I" wasn't doing it; "I" wasn't the one allowing it. There isn't a preference for something else to happen. If my heart still aches, my heart still aches.

The sadness will go away when it goes away. It does not matter to me the duration. I love you, Molly. Thank you so much for all the joy you brought me. What a teacher you were. I'll never forget how present and accepting you were.

Your sparkling, light brown eyes were so open and transparent, so full of affection and unconditional love. You are in my heart forever and I can never repay you for all you gave me.

When anger arises, it is allowed to arise. It's expressed without any self-consciousness, and then it subsides. No big deal. If there is a need to apologize, you simply apologize.

You don't automatically become a kinder, more loving person. That's just more myth piled on, so you can toss that notion aside.

This isn't about becoming a better person, because there was never any separate person present in the first place. When you know it's all one, you tend not to mistreat your Self.

All experience is welcome here, especially the unpleasant

Seeing Through The 12 Biggest Obstacles To Enlightenment

stuff.

Christian Mystic, Julian of Norwich, was innocently mistaken when she said, "All shall be well." The true pointer is, "All *is* well, even when it isn't."

Never take anyone else's word for truth, no matter how highly regarded that person is, no matter how high their chair is elevated, and no matter how many sit at and kiss their feet.

Once you start following someone else, you cease to follow truth.

Always confirm in your own direct experience what is true.

There are no stages or levels to enlightenment. I understand that some believe this just because someone they regard highly says so. This is a huge obstacle. Let it go.

Enlightenment is much simpler than that, and doesn't involve that.

That which is being pointed to here has nothing to do with the concept of stages or levels. Stages and levels are imagined ideas that imply time, and you are the time-less.

If what you are is time-less, space-less, and one without a second, how could stages and levels apply to the non-dual essence you are?

There is no progression in This That You Are.

If someone tells you that there are steps and stages to enlightenment, run from them.

If someone tells you, "I am enlightened", it just isn't true. There is no such thing as an enlightened person. Enlightenment is the complete absence of any person.

The idea of stages and levels are imagined in awareness, the stage-free, level-free, ever-present background of being. There is no need to travel anywhere, get to any level or stage in

Seeing Through The 12 Biggest Obstacles To Enlightenment

order to be who you already are, here and now.

There really is nothing to attain, gain or reach.

None of the great non-dual teachers in history (Jesus, Ramana, Nisargaddatta, Papaji, Dogen, Wu Hsin, Jean Klein, Bob Adamson and Buddha to name a few) ever spoke of levels of attainment, as they knew such ideas were created and sustained in the mind that can never realize this.

I assure you, the discovery of what you really are is much simpler than that. How can I say this? You can say this when all doubt has been removed, and since the questioner has been seen through, all questions have been extinguished.

You know that you know.

You are the simple and undeniable presence of awareness that is the backdrop of all experience. You are the welcoming, formless container in which all appearance comes and goes in, never obscured by thought, emotion, sensation or conditioning.

Nothing can obscure awareness. All obscurations appear in awareness; everything is registered clearly and cleanly, especially those things that appear muddy or confusing.

You are the Unborn that gives birth to the born. You are the unconditioned that gives rise to the conditioned.

There is only That – and You Are That.

There are those who believe that in order for enlightenment to 'happen' to them (nothing really happens, by the way) one must receive special instructions from an enlightened teacher, to you, the rare and chosen student.

This jive talk is perhaps my favorite kind of jive talk, mostly because it's humorous and brings out a chuckle in me. We can see how the mind would find this complete myth fascinating and true.

I'm sorry to break it to the fascinated minds out there that are still holding onto this idea, but there aren't any hidden esoteric schools in hidden Himalayan monasteries that contain the way to enlightenment. Perhaps you believe it because someone you (and others) hold in high regard said so.

And that's okay. Just drop this particular belief (and all others) and return to the open state of discovery, where you believe in nothing, where you know absolutely nothing...but only if you truly want to awaken.

Come bared-naked without any expectation, and without any demand - and empty your cup.

The simple recognition of your true nature, that which doesn't contain stages or levels, isn't as rare as you may think...

After all, You ARE the enlightenment you seek.

Chapter 12
A Sense of a Separate Self

There is no such thing as a person. There are only restrictions and limitations. The sum total of these defines the person. You think you know yourself when you know what you are. But you never know who you are. The person merely appears to be, like the space within the pot appears to have the shape and volume and smell of the pot. Like the space within the pot, see that you are not what you believe yourself to be.

~ Nisargadatta Maharaj

Soon after birth, the sense of a separate self arises. It is not a thought at this early stage; it's energetic and it's called self-consciousness. Aside from the human being, there is no other organism that possesses the ability to be self-conscious.

The moment the human believes in the idea of separation is the moment the "me" is born. From this point on, and for the rest of most people's lives, the "me" expends a lot of energy trying to make its life work by negotiating with everything under the sun.

Its primary motive is to move towards pleasure and away from pain. As long as there is this idea of separation, there will always be a sense that there is something missing. From this grasping and aversion perspective, we can't help but remain on the wheel of suffering.

All the while, every longing we have is longing to come home to the wholeness we already are. We aren't aware that we're looking to become whole through a veil of separation. Since the "me" is based in separation, wholeness will never be found.

Nonetheless, as I mentioned in "The Lazy Man's Way To Enlightenment", if it were not for the separate sense of self, you wouldn't know which mouth to feed when you were hungry, or which nose to scratch when you had an itch.

Having a separate sense of self is an operational necessity. Without it, we'd be set adrift in a sea of bodies, not knowing which body we are, unaware of which body to care for.

Despite what you may have heard, the separate sense of self does not leave your experience for good upon awakening. Since this is an important thing to see, let's get this one straight. You have to believe that the arising of a separate sense of self is problematic.

What tells you that it's problematic?

A thought tells you it is problematic, right?

When you believe this thought, then it *becomes* a problem. If you don't believe it, there is nothing to sustain it. Otherwise, you feed this notion that it's problematic by making it significant!

Is it really and truly significant, or is it just a thought that tells you it is really and truly significant?

We leave the rails when we conclude that if there is a sense of a separate self, then there must *be* a separate self.

This unexamined assumption is the cause of all our problems, and the erroneous premise upon which all other assumptions and premises are predicated.

Fortunately, in one fell swoop, in one clear and distinct recognition, this assumption crumbles in the light of truth.

Doubt, being the last thing to leave, evaporates in this unmistakable seeing, never to appear again.

Once we see through this Great Assumption that is the cause of all our problems, what must happen to the effects? What must happen to the effects that are generated by a false cause?

Dissolved. Erased. Gone. Finished.

This assumption was the very thing Buddha saw through.

This essential insight is the proverbial nail in the coffin insight that Buddhism was founded upon.

The primary aim of Buddhism isn't to create more Buddhists, but to create more Buddhas, awake and free!

But let's be honest here. It is pretty easy to see why this assumption takes place, isn't it? Isn't it very logical, rational and reasonable to believe that since there is a sense of a separate self, it must *mean* that there is a separate self?

Incidentally, these three components (logic, rationality and reason) are generally what the mind uses to reference truth or reality. And as we've discussed, what you are cannot be approached by these means. Mind can't approach what is beyond the mind.

And since it's not really the function and scope of the mind to go beyond appearances, it makes perfect sense it's overlooked. It makes perfect sense the mind will never see this.

I can tell you from direct experience that the simple realization of what you are is beyond all three, so if you're interested in the direct route, I encourage you not to rely on any of the three.

While I can report that the sense of self never really goes away for good (aside from deep sleep, meditation, Nirvikalpa Samadhi, occasional unitive experiences, etc) the sense of "my" and "mine" does.

In fact, the sense of "my" and "mine" completely vanishes.

When the "I" thought is clearly seen to be fictitious, this is what happens.

The author of this book went beyond the 'since there is a sense of a separate self, there must be a separate self' assumption and investigated whether it was true or not.

After all, all suffering and all problems hinge (and depend on) this investigation!

Pretty essential, don't you agree?

Now, I am reminding YOU of what YOU already know, but have simply forgotten, or have yet to see.

Once the seeing of what you really are has been stabilized, all of the feelings, thoughts, experiences and sensations that were associated with the 'me' of memory are completely obliterated.

And when you don't look NOW, it has to be the "me" of memory. When you look now, in direct experience, you won't find any such entity present.

Feelings, thoughts and sensations still go on as before, but without any identification with them as belonging to me.

Identification = stickiness, doubt and confusion.

Dis-identification = transparency, knowing and clarity.

If there is no separate entity present, who is there to claim them? The belief in the "me" as the center gets annihilated in the seeing that there never was a self that existed in the first place.

This very fact is the most overlooked thing in the history

of mankind. It's like mining for a diamond in your back yard, while having a diamond in your pocket all along.

You already are what you are looking for.

The mind can't ever see this. Oh, you should see the looks I get from family and friends when I attempt to describe the indescribable.

With truth seekers, you usually don't get those looks. Most get a sense of what you're saying.

No longer do you call life "yours." You never had a life. Life spontaneously unfolds within the impersonal awareness you are.

In this seeing, it is recognized that all life is simply a spontaneous appearance unfolding in the ever-present, presence of awareness that you are.

Absolutely everything that was referenced back to the "you" that you thought you were dissolves. All longings to be anything other than what you are vanish in the clear recognition of your Real Identity.

All doubt, insecurity, self-esteem issues and psychological and emotional issues are spontaneously resolved in the clear recognition that "you" never were.

To know and realize that You Are The Untouched Space Of Pure Spirit that welcomes all is wonderfully freeing.

To be clear, there is no event in time called enlightenment or awakening. Realizing what you already are is a simple recognition of what is already the case, eternally and outside the stream of time and events.

What you are is clearly seen and fully recognized and stabilizes – or what you are is not clearly seen and recognized. And yet nothing really "happens."

There is no one who needs to awaken. Don't get caught up in this pointer. If confusion arises, just look and see if the awareness of confusion is confused – and then rest in that.

The best part is that personal struggles and persistent issues don't arise again. Awareness has no problems and You are awareness.

Let all your stories go in the light of the radiant, problem-free awareness you are. See this and be free!

You don't become some holy or "more spiritual" person. You don't become super wise and ultra compassionate, either.

And most people won't know the difference in you, but who cares? Who needs the recognition? There is a deep humility that comes with this. After all, it is nothing "you" did, nor is it something "you" earned or attained.

You're being lived, so how can "you" take credit for anything?

Most things go on as before, but for no one. In comes the experience of being extremely comfortable in your own skin, and it's not even your skin!

Where once problems were sticky, now they're simply life conditions that pass through, because there is no one present to take ownership of them.

Self-centered thoughts are rooted in the belief that there is a self at the center. Once it is seen that there never was an entity present at the center, it's a done deal. No more psychological and emotional suffering – and no more seeking, either.

To be done with seeking is very strange indeed. In its place, there is a deep contentment that is hard to put into words. The desire to seek for truth completely drops away and it's very liberating to say the least. Residual habits of mind may still come up, but they aren't a problem anymore.

If they remain, they remain. No big deal for the one who isn't.

Seeing Through The 12 Biggest Obstacles To Enlightenment

Can identification still happen? Yes, from time to time and it isn't a problem. To borrow from one of Nisargaddata's favorite phrases, "it is seen through rather quickly and discarded."

It is the belief in the separate self as the reality that muddles the picture. It is the person that clogs up experience. Real clarity comes from recognizing the absence of the person.

There is absolutely nothing you need to do or practice to see this. Examine closely what you've heretofore neglected to examine. There is no magic in it and there is no special kind of looking involved.

Root out the false and the true remains.

The "answer" has been here all along, and when you finally investigate, it will be revealed.

When you really look and see that the snake really isn't a snake after all, fear of the snake automatically drops away once it is seen that it was a rope all along.

There has never been a separate person present – ever. If you think there is one present that is reading this book right now, please look and see if you can locate this entity you call you.

Don't just assume.

Aside from passing thoughts, sensations and emotion, is there any entity present that you can undoubtedly (and absolutely) call yourself? Stay with this and do not reference the mind to tell you what is so.

Without conceptualizing, stay with present and direct experience, and then tell the truth!

Present before thought, You are. See this and be done with the spiritual search.

Don't let this book just be another book on enlightenment and awakening that you've conceptually read and understood!

Seeing Through The 12 Biggest Obstacles To Enlightenment

Put the book down now and LOOK. I promise you, you won't find a thing.

If fear arises, let it arise. See that it temporarily arises in the ever-present, fear-less presence of awareness you are.

The sense of separation, the sense of being a separate "I" distinct from another separate "I" can only survive through NOT being investigated.

Because it has not been seen to be a complete fabrication (this imagined separation), it continues to be the cause of all your problems. An imagined entity causing imagined problems.

Pretty crazy, I agree.

You can't get rid of this belief, because the "you" that is trying to get rid of it is based on the actual sense of separation itself.

But fortunately, once it is clearly seen (by no one) that there never was a separate self at all, like a house of cards, it all collapses in clear seeing.

So go ahead, look again and see if you can find this separate self that you've believed in your entire life. And through this looking, notice the awareness that is vividly and undeniably present.

Awareness continues as the unchanging background of all sensing, perceiving and knowing. Awareness continues as the background to the idea you are a separate self.

Get out of your own way.

Relax and This That's Awake comes alive in You.

Stop deceiving yourself right now and see the truth.

THIS IS WHAT YOU ARE, THE PROBLEM-FREE AWARE PRESENCE that literally everything comes and goes in.

You are already free; you've always *been* free.

Seeing Through The 12 Biggest Obstacles To Enlightenment

Just see the facts as they are. No time is needed to see this, so put away your watches.

The root of all suffering (the belief in a separate individual) is nothing other than a mistaken assumption. It's that simple.

There is no such entity to be found in direct experience, so do not ignore direct experience.

The notion of being a separate "I" is simply false. See the false as false and the truth sets you free.

See this and return home to the place you never left.

After all, there is no place like Home.

No one can do this for you. Nothing is more rewarding.

Now, it's your turn.

In A Nutshell

Whether its been realized or not, YOU are the Formless Light of Consciousness, the ONE REALITY, the aware presence that absolutely everything appears in. This unbounded space is the basis, the substratum and ground of all sensory experience and yet, it is beyond the senses. Some call this Spirit, but it doesn't matter what you call it because the word is never the actual. You are both Nothing and Everything, both Empty and Full. There is no mind apart from thinking. When thinking stops, you still ARE. You can't know or find what you are; you can only realize and BE what you are. Only an object can be known and You are the Subject that knows objects. No path or journey is needed to see and be what you already and always are. Consciously BE what you really are, or unconsciously pretend to be who you think you are. You were never born and you will never die. Birth and death are mere concepts arising in the actuality of what you are. Nothing is apart from what You are, and everything IS because of what you ARE. There is no one who needs to awaken or attain enlightenment. What YOU really are is already free, fully awake and present. SEE this. There are no real obstacles to seeing this, only seeming ones. What you are still IS no matter what you do, no matter what you see or don't see. Wake up from the dream of separation and realize what you are!

Made in the USA
Lexington, KY
01 April 2015